AF674211

Bhagavad Gita
Life Lessons
and Insights
for Children
Stories and Plays For Teachers and Students

BHAGAVAD GITA LIFE LESSONS AND INSIGHTS FOR CHILDREN

Language: English

Date of Publication: 24 March 2025

Price: $ 30 (USD) (Thirty Dollars)

30

ISBN: 978-93-342-7815-6

9 789334 278156

Author/Editor: Nagashwini N
Copyright © 2025 by Nagashwini N. All rights reserved.

First Edition.

Published by: Nagashwini N
#23, 5th 'A' Main Road, Obalappa Garden,
BENGALURU, KARNATAKA, INDIA.

Disclaimer

This book is a **creative and educational adaptation** of the teachings of the *Bhagavad Gita*, presented through **modern allegories, fictional characters, and dramatized storytelling** for the understanding of young readers.

The characters, settings, and stories are **inspired by the values and messages** found in the original scripture but are **not direct translations or theological commentaries**. The intent is to help children explore **moral choices, inner strength, and self-awareness** in a relatable, age-appropriate way.

These interpretations are **not affiliated with any particular religious or spiritual organization**. They are meant to inspire **positive thinking, reflection, and open discussion** among readers of all backgrounds.

All stories are fictional. Any resemblance to real people, living or dead, is purely coincidental. The teachings and lessons shared here are **metaphorical** and should not be taken as justifications for actions that harm oneself or others.

Parents and educators are encouraged to **read along with children** and support them in discussing and applying the values of **wisdom, courage, humility, and compassion** in their everyday life.

Preface

The *Bhagavad Gita*, a timeless spiritual classic, has inspired millions across generations with its profound teachings on duty, values, courage, and the path of righteous living. While traditionally studied by adults and scholars, its core messages—when adapted through stories and plays—hold immense value for children as well.

This book, *Bhagavad Gita: Life Lessons and Insights for Children*, is specially crafted for young minds, curious hearts, and nurturing adults. It is a humble attempt to make the wisdom of the Gita accessible, relatable, and enjoyable for children through engaging stories and simple dramatizations. Each story and play draws from the Gita's chapters and teachings, and connects them with everyday challenges children face—friendship, honesty, fear, decision-making, responsibility, and perseverance.

Teachers can use these plays in classrooms to promote discussions on values. Parents can read the stories with their children to foster meaningful conversations. Children can perform these short skits, reflect on the questions at the end, and discover how ancient wisdom is still alive in their modern lives.

May this book serve as a bridge between timeless philosophy and youthful imagination, encouraging children to think deeply, act wisely, and grow with purpose.

With reverence and love,
Nagashwini N

Table of Contents

Introduction

Introduction to the Bhagavad Gita and the Kurukshetra War

Long ago, in ancient India, there was a great kingdom called **Bharata**, ruled by noble kings and warriors. Among them were two sets of royal cousins – the **Kauravas** and the **Pandavas**. They were part of the same royal family but had many conflicts over justice, honor, and the right to rule the kingdom of **Hastinapura**.

The tension between them grew stronger with time, and after failed attempts at peace, it led to a huge war — the **Kurukshetra War**.

This war was not just an ordinary battle. It was a war of righteousness (**Dharma**) versus injustice (**Adharma**). On one side were the **Pandavas**, five heroic brothers led by **Yudhishthira**, and on the other side were the **Kauravas**, a hundred brothers led by **Duryodhana**.

Just before the war began, on the battlefield of **Kurukshetra**, something very special happened.

One of the Pandava brothers, the mighty archer **Arjuna**, saw his relatives, teachers, and friends standing on both sides, ready to fight and die. His heart was filled with sorrow and confusion. He dropped his bow and said, **"I cannot fight this war. What is the use of killing my own people?"**

At that moment, **Lord Krishna**, who was Arjuna's friend and charioteer, spoke to him with deep wisdom and truth. These divine teachings, spoken by Krishna to Arjuna on the battlefield, are known as the **Bhagavad Gita** — which means **"The Song of God."**

What is the Bhagavad Gita?

- The **Bhagavad Gita** is part of the **Mahabharata**, written by the sage **Vyasa**.
- It appears in the **Bhishma Parva (Book of Bhishma)**, in chapters 23 to 40 of the Mahabharata.
- It contains **18 chapters and 700 verses**.
- It is a dialogue between **Arjuna and Krishna**.
- The Gita explains deep truths about life, duty, courage, selflessness, the soul, and devotion.

Why is the Bhagavad Gita Important?

The Gita is not just about war. It is a **guide for life**. It teaches us:

- How to do our **duty** without selfishness.
- How to face **challenges** with courage.
- How to **control the mind and emotions**.
- How to live with **wisdom, devotion, and peace**.

Chapter 1

Title1: "The Big Debate: Aryan's Choice"

Characters:

- **Aryan** – A bright, kind-hearted 13-year-old boy (Arjuna)
- **Grandpa Veer** – Wise and calm grandfather (Krishna)
- **The Mindfield School Hall** – Represents the battlefield (Kurukshetra)
- **Doubt, Fear, Confusion** – Imaginary characters in Aryan's mind
- **Friends: Dev, Meena, Riya, Karan** – Classmates, some supportive, some mocking
- **Principal Dharma** – The authority figure representing justice

Scene 1: The Mindfield School Hall (The Battlefield)

(The school is hosting the Annual Leadership Debate Competition. Aryan has been chosen to represent his class. The stage is set. His friends cheer him on, but Aryan stands behind the curtain, nervous.)

Dev (cheering): "Go Aryan! You're going to win this one, buddy!"

Riya: "Just speak from your heart. You're the best speaker in school!"

Karan (mocking): "Let's see if the class genius chokes on stage today!"

(Aryan hears all voices but his mind is not calm. Suddenly, time freezes. The lights dim. Three characters appear—Doubt, Fear, and Confusion. They are dressed in black with smoky edges.)

Scene 2: Aryan's Inner World (The Battlefield of the Mind)

Doubt (laughing): "You? Speak? What if you forget everything on stage?"

Fear (echoing): "What if they laugh at you? What if you make a mistake?"

Confusion (whispering): "Why even debate? It may hurt someone's feelings. Maybe just give up..."

(Aryan clutches his chest and sits down backstage. Just then, Grandpa Veer walks in calmly, holding a thermos of hot chocolate.)

Scene 3: Conversation with Grandpa Veer (Krishna's Role)

Grandpa Veer (gently): "Aryan, what's the matter, my brave warrior?"

Aryan (with tears): "I can't do this, Grandpa. My friends… some cheer me, some tease me. I feel I'll mess it up. What if I hurt someone's feelings with my arguments? I don't want to fight!"

Grandpa Veer (smiling): "Ah… this is not just a debate stage, Aryan. It's your **Mindfield**. And these voices… they are your **inner enemies**. You are standing at the edge of an important battle—not outside—but inside your own heart."

Scene 4: The Teaching Moment (Krishna's Message)

Grandpa Veer:
"Let me tell you something the wise have always known. You are not just a body with fear, doubt, and confusion. You are a strong,

wise soul—full of courage and purpose.
Just like the warrior Arjuna on the battlefield, you are torn between right and wrong.
But always remember—**your duty, your dharma**, is to try with your whole heart, not to run away from the challenge."

Aryan: "But what if I fail?"

Grandpa Veer: "Success or failure doesn't matter. What matters is that you showed up, you spoke your truth, and you stood tall. That is real winning."

Scene 5: Back on the Stage (Resolution)

(Aryan walks on stage, his back straight, eyes glowing with courage. The imaginary voices vanish. The spotlight shines. He looks into the crowd and smiles.)

Aryan (to the audience):
"I stand here not to fight against my friends,
but to stand up for what I believe in.
I may be nervous, I may make mistakes,
but I will not let fear rule me today!"

(Thunderous applause. Grandpa Veer smiles in the crowd. Principal Dharma nods with pride.)

Moral of the Story:

"True bravery is not fighting others, but fighting our own doubts, fears, and

confusion. When we perform our duty with courage and a clear heart, we become heroes in the battlefield of the mind."

Allegory Table:

Bhagavad Gita	Modern Story
Arjuna	Aryan, the student
Krishna	Grandpa Veer
Kurukshetra battlefield	School stage & inner mind
Kauravas (attachments, doubts)	Doubt, fear, confusion
Dharma (duty)	Speaking truthfully in the debate
Arjuna's dilemma	Aryan's hesitation
Krishna's guidance	Grandpa's wisdom
War	Internal struggle with fear and duty

Chapter 1

Title1a: "The Final Match: A Battle of Choices"

Characters:

- **Arjun (Aarav)** – a brilliant but confused student
- **Krishna (Krish Sir)** – a wise school mentor
- **Dhritarashtra (Principal Dhiraj)** – the blind (emotionally) school principal
- **Duryodhana (Dheeraj)** – Aarav's rival and class monitor
- **Bheeshma (Mr. Bhaskar)** – the strict senior teacher who supports Dheeraj
- **Dronacharya (Mr. Dev)** – Aarav's former teacher, now favoring the rival group

- **The Pandava Team** – Aarav's teammates, including his brothers and friends
- **The Kaurava Team** – the rival debate team, full of school's top scorers but arrogant

Scene 1: The Grand Debate Arena

(Setting: A big hall with two sides – left for Aarav's team and right for Dheeraj's team. The school is holding its final debate competition – the "Battle of Wisdom.")

Principal Dhiraj (monologuing, represents Dhritarashtra – Verse 1):
"Sanjay (the commentator), what's happening on the stage between my son Dheeraj's team and Aarav's team?"
(Blind to fairness, he is more interested in how his son wins.)

Allegory: Dhritarashtra represents *spiritual blindness*, being more attached to his son than to truth.

Scene 2: Duryodhana's Arrogant Whisper

Dheeraj (pulling Mr. Bhaskar aside):
"Sir, our team is the best! But just in case, let's play it smart. Aarav's team has Krish Sir mentoring them. That's dangerous."

Allegory (Verse 2-11): Duryodhana trying to outwit wisdom. Arrogance tries to strategize against dharma (righteousness).

Scene 3: The Warriors Assemble

Mr. Dev (walking over):
"I trained both teams. But Aarav lacks confidence now. He'll break under pressure."

Mr. Bhaskar:
"Let's announce the beginning with a clap of wisdom!"
(He rings the bell like Bheeshma blowing the conch.)

Allegory (Verse 12-19): Trumpets of war represent inner conflicts rising before a big decision.

Scene 4: Aarav Feels the Heat

Krish Sir (calmly):
"Aarav, look at both teams. Observe and reflect."

Aarav (nervous):
"They're all my friends, my cousins… even my old teachers. How can I debate against them?"
(He starts sweating and trembling.)

Allegory (Verse 20-27): Arjuna asking Krishna to place the chariot in the middle—means seeing life from the center of conflict. He sees attachments and relationships creating confusion.

Scene 5: Aarav's Meltdown

Aarav (voice trembling):
"Krish Sir, I can't do this! My voice is shaking… my brain feels frozen. I don't want to hurt anyone. I give up!"
(He drops the mic. Everyone gasps.)

Krish Sir (firm yet calm):
"Aarav, sit down. Observe your feelings. This is your battle of self-discovery."

Allegory (Verse 28-47): Arjuna's emotional breakdown symbolizes the *inner war* of doubt, guilt, and attachment.

End of Chapter 1 Story – Curtain Falls

Moral of the Story:

Sometimes, life puts us in situations where we must choose between right and wrong, even if it means going against people we care about. Avoiding the problem doesn't solve it. Recognizing your inner confusion is the first step toward clarity.

Allegory Table:

Gita Verse	Modern Allegory	Metaphor

1.1	Principal Dhiraj is blind to fairness	Spiritual blindness (Dhritarashtra)
1.2–11	Dheeraj tries to manipulate teachers	Ego and strategy against dharma
1.12–1.19	Teachers blow whistles and ring bells	Emotional signals before inner conflict
1.20–1.27	Aarav sees friends and mentors on both sides	Attachments confuse decision-making
1.28–1. 47	Aarav breaks down and drops the mic	Emotional paralysis, fear of duty

Kids' Insights & Takeaways

1. **Courage isn't the absence of fear** – it's choosing to move forward despite it.
2. **Sometimes doing the right thing feels uncomfortable**, especially when friends or family are involved.
3. **Avoiding decisions doesn't make problems disappear**.
4. **Feelings are okay** – even great heroes like Arjuna (or Aarav) feel fear.

5. **There is always a Krish Sir (a guide) in our life** who can help us see clearly.

Chapter 2

Title2: "Aryan's Awakening: The Wise Within"

Characters:

- **Aryan** – The same 13-year-old student (Arjuna)
- **Grandpa Veer** – The wise guide (Krishna)
- **Voices in Aryan's Mind:**
    - **Fear** – Represents fear of failure
    - **Ego** – Arrogance and pride
    - **Doubt** – Self-questioning and confusion
- **Principal Dharma** – Authority of justice
- **Friends: Dev, Meena, Riya** – Support system

- **Timekeeper** – Represents Time, always ticking

Scene 1: Aryan's Confusion Returns (Verse 2.2, 2.3)

(Aryan wins the debate. Applause fades. Days pass. Now he's asked to lead a school project. A big one. Suddenly, he's scared again.)

Aryan (to himself): "What if I fail this time? Debate was different. This is harder."

(Fear, Ego, and Doubt appear like shadows again.)

Fear: "This time you'll fall. Everyone's watching!"

Ego: "If you can't be perfect, don't even try."

Doubt: "You're not ready. Better step back."

(Aryan hides behind the library shelf. Grandpa Veer enters silently.)

Grandpa Veer (sternly, like Krishna in 2.2): "Where is this weakness from, Aryan? This fear does not suit a leader. Stand tall! You were not born to run away like this!"

Scene 2: The Unshakable You (Verse 2.13, 2.20)

Grandpa Veer (sitting beside Aryan):
"Aryan, do you think you are just this body that fears and shivers?"

Aryan: "But I *feel* weak, Grandpa…"

Grandpa Veer:
"The body changes—like your school uniforms from class to class. But the 'real you' inside—the soul—is forever. It doesn't get scared. It doesn't get tired. It never dies. Just like you move from one grade to the next, your soul moves through life, ever strong, ever calm."

(Suddenly, a dreamlike vision appears: Aryan as a toddler, then younger, then present. In all stages, his soul remains the same glowing figure.)

Scene 3: Like Changing Clothes (Verse 2.22)

Grandpa Veer:
"Think of your body as your clothes. When they're worn out, you don't cry. You simply change them."

Aryan (softly): "So... if I'm not this fear, I don't need to listen to it?"

Grandpa Veer (smiling):
"Exactly. Listen to your wise self inside, not these noisy shadows."

(Fear, Ego, and Doubt begin shrinking.)

Scene 4: The Equanimous Mind (Verse 2.47 & 2.50)

(Later, Aryan starts working on the project. He messes up a drawing. His group laughs a little.)

Aryan (frustrated): "Ugh! I failed!"

Grandpa Veer (appearing like magic again): "Aryan, remember—**do your duty, not for the result**. You're not the owner of the prize. Your job is to try. This balance of mind is called *Yoga*."

Aryan (nodding): "So I should focus on effort, not awards?"

Grandpa Veer:
"Yes. That makes your mind calm, like a still lake, even when stones of failure or success are thrown in."

Scene 5: A Wise Warrior Rises (Verse 2.70)

(Days later. The project ends. Aryan didn't win the school prize. But he smiles as he watches his classmates clapping for another team.)

Principal Dharma (announcing):
"Aryan's group may not have won, but his leadership, calm, and teamwork made the biggest difference."

(Aryan bows. Grandpa Veer appears behind the crowd and nods with pride.)

Grandpa Veer (in Aryan's mind):
"Like the ocean that stays full even as rivers flow into it, a wise one stays steady whether success or failure comes."

Moral of the Story:

"You are not the body or emotions, but the wise soul within. Do your duty with calmness. Let go of results. Win or lose, your effort is your victory."

Allegory Table:

Verse	Gita Teaching	Story Element
2.2 & 2.3	Reject weakness and rise like a warrior	Grandpa Veer urges Aryan to stop hiding
2.13	Soul moves through life stages	Aryan sees his soul through his ages
2.20	Soul is eternal, never born nor dead	Aryan realizes fear can't touch his soul
2.22	Soul changes bodies like clothes	Visual metaphor of changing uniforms
2.47	Do your duty, not for results	Aryan continues the project calmly

2.50	Yoga is skill in action	Aryan finds peace in trying his best
2.70	Be steady amidst gain or loss	Aryan feels happy, prize or no prize

Chapter 2

Title2a: "The Wisdom Coach: Winning from Within"

Characters:

- **Aarav (Arjuna)** – the confused student
- **Krish Sir (Krishna)** – the wise coach and mentor
- **Principal Dhiraj (Dhritarashtra)** – the partial authority
- **Dheeraj (Duryodhana)** – the rival student
- **Friends, teachers, crowd, classmates** – spectators of the big moment.

Scene 1: Aarav Sits on the Floor, Mic Dropped (Verses 1-12)

(Krish Sir stands near Aarav, who is sitting on the debate stage with his head down.)

Krish Sir: “Aarav, why this sadness? You’re a warrior of words, not a runner from truth. Get up!”

Aarav: “But I don’t want to hurt anyone. What’s the point if I lose my peace?”

Krish Sir (calmly): “This moment isn’t about hurting, it’s about choosing what’s right. You speak as if you're wise, but you are shaken by emotions.”

Allegory: Arjuna’s sorrow represents inner confusion. Krishna begins teaching – not just debating with logic, but waking up the soul.

Scene 2: The Real Self Never Dies (Verses 13–30)

Krish Sir (standing with hands folded): “Aarav, do you know what never dies?”

Aarav (confused): “What do you mean? Everyone dies one day…”

Krish Sir (smiling): “Our body changes like school uniforms through the year – but our true self, our soul, is like the student inside. Clothes change. The student doesn’t.”

Aarav: “So… even if someone loses, they aren’t really lost?”

Krish Sir: "Exactly! You're fighting for truth, not for trophies. The soul isn't harmed by words or failure."

Allegory: The body is temporary. The soul is eternal. Like changing roles in school or clothes – the 'real you' doesn't change.

Scene 3: Do Your Duty Without Fear (Verses 31–38)

Krish Sir: "You have a role here, Aarav. Running away is not noble. This debate is your dharma—your duty."

Aarav: "But what if I lose? Or hurt someone?"

Krish Sir: "Success or failure, win or lose – don't let results scare you. Play your part. You're not here to win over people, but over your own fear."

Allegory: Dharma means doing your responsibility. Fear of result blocks us. Let go of result-thinking and focus on doing the right thing.

Scene 4: The Steady Mind (Verses 39–53)

Krish Sir (takes a whiteboard):
"Now listen, Aarav. This is *Buddhi Yoga* – training the mind. A wise person doesn't get super happy when praised or broken when criticized. Stay steady."

Aarav (nodding): "You mean... not to depend on how people react?"

Krish Sir: "Yes! Be like the deep ocean – waves above, but calm inside."

Allegory: A steady mind is the goal. Don't be a balloon flying with every compliment or falling with every insult.

Scene 5: The Signs of a Wise One (Verses 54–72)

Aarav: "Sir, how does a truly wise person behave?"

Krish Sir: "They speak less, listen more. They aren't too attached to things. They don't chase pleasure or run from pain. Like a mountain—calm and still."

Aarav: "So I must learn to be still inside?"

Krish Sir: "Yes, Aarav. Real victory is not outside. It's mastering your inner world."

Final Scene: Aarav Stands Up

Aarav (slowly rising):
"I understand now. I was afraid of the storm outside, but the real storm was inside me. I will face it, Sir."

Krish Sir: "Well spoken. Now go, not to defeat others, but to awaken the real you."

Crowd applauds as Aarav picks up the mic again with new strength.

Allegory Table:

Gita Verse	Modern Allegory	Metaphor
2.1–2.12	Krish Sir questions Aarav's grief	Grief from confusion, not wisdom
2.13–2.30	Clothes vs. Soul analogy, changing uniforms	Body is temporary, soul eternal
2.31–2.38	Aarav's role in the debate is his duty	Dharma (role/duty) over emotions
2.39–2.53	Teachings on balanced mind, deep ocean, balloon	Detachment from results, be like the ocean
2.54–2.72	Marks of a wise one – like a mountain	Peace is inner strength, stillness in action

Kids' Insights & Takeaways:

1. **You are more than your marks or clothes – your soul is unchanging.**

2. **Doing your duty matters more than winning or losing.**
3. **Don't let people's praise or criticism shake you – stay like the ocean.**
4. **A wise person stays calm even in chaos.**
5. **True courage is facing your inner fear, not running from responsibility.**

Chapter 3

Title3: "The Invisible Engine: Aryan's Karma Mission"

Characters:

- **Aryan** – The bright student leader (Arjuna)
- **Grandpa Veer** – The wise guide (Krishna)
- **Miss Karma** – Aryan's science teacher, symbolizes universal action
- **Lazyboy** – Aryan's inner voice of laziness and procrastination
- **Friends: Meena, Dev, Riya** – Teammates in the school community project
- **Principal Dharma** – The head of the school, promotes value-based learning

Scene 1: The School Garden Mess (Verse 3.5)

(It's the next term. Principal Dharma launches a new campaign called "Green School Mission." Every student team must clean and care for part of the garden.)

Miss Karma:
"Everyone must act. Nobody can stay idle. Even the Earth spins without stopping!"

Aryan (frowning): "Why can't we just rest during the break?"

(Suddenly, a lazy, stretchy character named Lazyboy appears in Aryan's mind.)

Lazyboy: "Shhh! Just skip it. Others will do the work. You deserve a nap!"

Grandpa Veer (arriving with a garden spade):
"Aryan, action is life itself. Even blinking, breathing, growing—everything is movement. Not working is also an action, but it leads to rusting, not shining."

Scene 2: Confusion Between Thinking and Doing (Verse 3.6, 3.7)

Aryan (sighing): "But Grandpa, sometimes I just *think* about doing things. That counts, right?"

Grandpa Veer:
"Hmm. Imagine a lamp that *thinks* of lighting up but never does. Is it useful?"

Aryan: "Nope..."

Grandpa Veer (chuckling):
"Then stop pretending to work in your head. True action comes from hands, heart, and effort—not daydreams."

Scene 3: Working Without Wanting Rewards (Verse 3.9)

(Aryan begins working. At first, he does it for praise. He expects a medal.)

Aryan: "Meena, when do they announce the Best Worker Award?"

Grandpa Veer (leaning on a rake):
"Aryan, if you do it only for the prize, your action becomes sticky like sugar syrup. But if you work without selfish desire, your work becomes pure and powerful—like fire that lights others."

Aryan: "So I should just do it... because it's right?"

Grandpa Veer: "Yes. Selfless action is sacred."

Scene 4: Following Duty – Not Others (Verse 3.35)

(Aryan looks at another team doing less work and still laughing.)

Aryan (whispering): "They're goofing off and still praised. Maybe we should do the same."

Grandpa Veer (firmly):
"Better to do your own work imperfectly than copy someone else's perfectly. Every soul has its path."

Aryan: "Even if it's harder?"

Grandpa Veer: "That's what makes it meaningful."

Scene 5: Action Inspires Others (Verse 3.21)

(Aryan continues working with a smile. Soon, other students notice.)

Riya: "Look! Aryan's group planted 15 saplings!"

Dev: "Let's go help them!"

(One by one, the school garden begins to bloom. Aryan unknowingly becomes a role model.)

Grandpa Veer:
"When leaders act with sincerity, others follow. You've become the silent engine, Aryan."

Scene 6: Understanding Karma as Worship (Verse 3.10–3.12)

Miss Karma (smiling):
"When you do your duty for the world, the world gives back. The plants you care for will give you air, joy, and color."

Aryan (softly):
"So… work is like worship?"

Grandpa Veer:
"Exactly. Work done in the spirit of service becomes holy."

Moral of the Story:

"True happiness comes from selfless action. Don't wait for reward—just act with heart, and you become the silent engine of change."

Allegory Table:

Verse	**Gita Teaching**	**Story Element**
3.5	No one can remain inactive, action is nature	Lazyboy vs garden duty
3.6, 3.7	Pretending to act is not real action	Aryan daydreaming about helping
3.9	Selfless action purifies	Aryan stops craving medals
3.21	Great people inspire others	Aryan becomes a silent role model

3.35	Better to follow your own path	Aryan avoids copying lazy teams
3.10–3.12	Duty as an offering, the cycle of nature	Garden giving back as a symbol of Karma cycle

Chapter 3

Title3a: "The Magic of Doing: Aarav's New Mission"

Main Characters:

- **Aarav (Arjuna)** – the curious student learning about life
- **Krish Sir (Krishna)** – the wise school mentor and life coach
- **Sneha (Sister)** – Aarav's younger sister who watches and learns
- **Class Monitor Group** – friends representing "doers"
- **The Lazy Gang** – students who try to avoid responsibilities
- **Mr. Karma** – the mysterious school helper (symbolic role)

Scene 1: Confused Again (Verses 1–8)

Aarav (scratching his head): "Krish Sir, earlier you told me knowledge is important. Now you're saying I must act. Which one is better – thinking or doing?"

Krish Sir (smiling gently): "Both are important, Aarav. But action is the path for most people. You can't learn to swim by only reading a book. You have to *jump in the pool*."

Allegory: Knowing without doing is like a seed that's never planted. Action gives knowledge life.

Scene 2: Can't Escape Work! (Verses 9–16)

Krish Sir: "Every job done with the right spirit is a kind of worship. Even sweeping the floor can be sacred if done selflessly."

Mr. Karma (sweeping the school courtyard, smiling silently)
—symbolizes the **invisible power of selfless action**.

Aarav (watching him): "He works every day without anyone noticing…"

Krish Sir: "He doesn't need praise. He serves for the joy of it. Work done for others keeps the world moving, like gears in a machine."

Allegory: Selfless action = Yajna (sacrifice). The world runs because people do their part without selfishness.

Scene 3: Aarav the Role Model (Verses 17–26)

Sneha (to Aarav): "I saw you cleaning the class even when no one told you to. Why?"

Aarav: "Because it's the right thing to do."

Krish Sir (stepping in): "Leaders must act as examples. Even if they don't need to, they do—so others are inspired."

Allegory: Even wise ones keep working to set an example. Role models act selflessly.

Scene 4: Enemies Within (Verses 27–35)

Lazy Gang (to Aarav): "Why do *you* bother? You're not the class monitor!"

Aarav: "I don't act because I *have* to. I act because it's *right*."

Krish Sir: "The real enemy isn't outside – it's inside: **desire** and **selfishness**. If you don't master them, they master you."

Allegory: Desire is like fire – it grows unless controlled. Don't let it rule your actions.

Final Scene: The Karma Awakening

Mr. Karma (finally speaks):
"You cannot escape doing. Even sitting idle is an action. Choose your actions wisely. Do your duty and let go of the reward."

Aarav (with a spark in his eyes):
"I get it now. Action is like magic—when done right, it changes the world, and me!"

Krish Sir: "Exactly. That's Karma Yoga. You've started your real journey."

Allegory Table:

Verse Range	Modern Allegory	Metaphor
3.1–3.8	Aarav confused about thought vs. action	Thinking is not enough without doing
3.9–3.16	Mr. Karma works silently as an example	Selfless work as sacrifice (Yajna)
3.17–3.26	Aarav inspires others through his actions	Leaders act to guide others
3.27–3.35	Desire as the hidden enemy	Inner fire of selfishness must be mastered

Kids' Insights & Takeaways:

1. **Action is powerful** – Doing the right thing is better than only thinking about it.

2. **Work can be worship** – Even small tasks matter when done with a good heart.
3. **Set examples for others** – People follow actions more than words.
4. **Desire and laziness are tricky enemies** – Don't let them control you.
5. **The world works because people do their part selflessly. Be one of them!**

Chapter 4

Title4: "The Time Capsule: Aryan Unlocks the Wisdom Code"

Main Characters:

- **Aryan** – The ever-curious 13-year-old (Arjuna)
- **Grandpa Veer** – The wise guide (Krishna)
- **Professor Veda** – A visiting guest who teaches "Wisdom through Time"
- **The Knowledge Scroll** – Magical object symbolizing timeless truth
- **Shadow of Ignorance** – A dark figure that creates confusion and doubt
- **Timekeeper** – Personification of Time
- **Classmates: Meena, Dev, Riya**

Scene 1: The Time Traveler's Entry (Verse 4.1–4.2)

(The school is buzzing. A special guest, Professor Veda, arrives to conduct a workshop titled "The Secret Wisdom Passed Through Time.")

Professor Veda (to students):
"Do you think great truths are new? No. Just like the sun rises again and again, truth is passed down—from wise to wise, through time."

Aryan (whispering): "Truth passed down… like a relay race?"

Grandpa Veer (appearing behind):
"Exactly! I gave this wisdom to those before you, Aryan. And now, you must receive it and pass it forward."

Scene 2: Aryan's Doubt and the Magic Scroll (Verse 4.4–4.6)

Aryan (confused):
"But Grandpa… how can *you* say you gave it before? You're right here with me now!"

(Suddenly, a magical scroll glows in his hands—"The Knowledge Scroll.")

Grandpa Veer (smiling):
"I've taken many forms, Aryan, just like the

same teacher comes in different uniforms across grades. I appear again and again when truth needs protecting."

*(The **Timekeeper** bows as Grandpa Veer steps forward.)*

Timekeeper:
"He appears when Dharma fades… to remind the world."

Scene 3: Secret of Selfless Action (Verse 4.13–4.14)

(Aryan starts using his garden work to teach younger students. He doesn't want credit.)

Meena: "Why don't you ever mention your name, Aryan?"

Aryan: "Because it's not about me. It's about what's right."

Grandpa Veer:
"When action is done with no ego, it becomes divine. Just like fire gives heat without desire, your action becomes pure when you let go of 'me' and 'mine.'"

Scene 4: Destroying Doubt with Knowledge (Verse 4.34 & 4.38)

(Aryan begins to question: What if he's still wrong? What if he's being used? Suddenly, the

***Shadow of Ignorance** creeps into his thoughts.)*

Shadow:
"You're just a kid. What do you know? Let the grownups handle truth."

Aryan (to Grandpa): "How do I know what's right?"

Grandpa Veer:
"Go to the truly wise—not those who only speak, but those who *live* wisdom. Ask with humility. Serve. Learn. Knowledge is the fire that burns ignorance."

(The Knowledge Scroll lights up and burns away the Shadow.)

Grandpa Veer (placing hand on Aryan's head):
"When doubt is gone, action becomes clear like a sunny sky after a storm."

Scene 5: Becoming a Wisdom Warrior (Verse 4.42)

(Aryan now walks confidently. He teaches, works, and acts without fear or pride.)

Grandpa Veer:
"Take the sword of knowledge and cut the knot of doubt. Arise, young seeker! Be a warrior of light!"

Aryan (standing tall):
"From today, I'll act in truth, share what I know, and learn from those wiser than me."

(The Scroll rolls itself up and flies into the sky. Aryan's notebook now glows on its own.)

Moral of the Story:

"True knowledge is not just about learning—it is about living it. When you act without ego and doubt, you become a warrior of wisdom."

Allegory Table:

Verse	Teaching	Story Element
4.1–4.2	Eternal wisdom passed down over time	Professor Veda, the scroll, time relay metaphor
4.4–4.6	God appears again and again to restore truth	Grandpa Veer's time-travel identity
4.13–4.14	Actions done without ego do not bind	Aryan helping students quietly
4.34	Learn from the wise with humility	Aryan approaching Grandpa Veer for wisdom
4.38	Knowledge purifies like fire	Scroll burns away Shadow of Ignorance

4.42	Cut doubt with wisdom and rise	Aryan becomes confident, ready to act

Chapter 4

Title4a: "The Secret of the Timeless Teacher"

Characters:

1. **Aryan** – A 13-year-old curious and thoughtful boy (represents Arjuna)
2. **Grandpa Ved** – A wise and calm grandfather who is secretly a retired scientist and philosopher (represents Krishna)
3. **Maya** – Aryan's best friend, practical and always asking tough questions
4. **Ms. Shraddha** – Their school teacher who gives the students a research project
5. **Timekeeper (symbolic)** – Mysterious figure appearing in dreams, represents timeless wisdom

6. **School Principal** – Represents the world's rules and expectations

Theme:

The story explores **how true knowledge transforms action**, and how doing one's duty selflessly with understanding is the path to peace and purpose. It also explains the mystery of timeless wisdom, the balance of action and renunciation, and the importance of **learning from a teacher**.

Scene 1: "The Impossible Project"

Setting: Classroom

(Inspired by verses 1–3 – Krishna explains he taught the Gita long ago to the Sun god)

Ms. Shraddha:
"Class, your final project is to uncover the *oldest wisdom* that still guides people today. It can be scientific, spiritual, or historical."

Aryan (whispering):
"How can wisdom from thousands of years ago still help us today?"

Maya:
"We need a living Google. Someone who has *lived* through time."

Narration:
That night, Aryan dreams of a strange glowing figure called the **Timekeeper**.

Timekeeper:
"The oldest truths are not stored in libraries. They are *lived*. Ask the Timeless Teacher."

Scene 2: "The Secret Identity"

Setting: Grandpa Ved's Garden

(Inspired by verses 4–9 – Krishna reveals his divine nature and incarnations)

Aryan:
"Grandpa, how can someone teach something before they're even born?"

Grandpa Ved (smiling):
"Because truth is beyond time. A wise one returns again and again, not to show off, but to lift others up."

Maya:
"Wait—are you saying you've done this before?"

Grandpa Ved (laughs mysteriously):
"I've worn many hats, child. The point is not who I am, but what you learn."

Narration:
Aryan realizes that knowledge isn't about age. It's about wisdom being reborn in every era through those who *act selflessly*.

Scene 3: "Fire of Knowledge"

Setting: Grandpa Ved's Study Room – books, diagrams, fire simulation model

(Inspired by verses 10–19 – Selfless action & knowledge burns away karma)

Grandpa Ved:
"Knowledge is like fire. It burns away confusion. When you act without selfishness, your actions leave no stains."

Aryan:
"But how do I know if I'm being selfish?"

Grandpa Ved:
"When you ask: 'How can I help?' instead of 'What do I get?' – you're on the right path."

Maya:
"So... even school homework can be spiritual?"

Grandpa Ved:
"Yes, if done with devotion and purpose."

Scene 4: "The Many Paths"

Setting: School Science Fair

(Inspired by verses 20–28 – Various kinds of yajnas or sacrifices of knowledge, study, austerity)

Narration:
The students build a "Path of Sacrifice" maze to explain how people offer different things—food, time, effort, or study—as part of their learning.

Principal:
"This project is unusual... but brilliant! You've shown that sacrifice isn't only about giving things away, but also giving up *ego*."

Aryan (to Maya):
"We didn't just do a project. We offered our best effort. That *was* our yajna."

Scene 5: "Learning from the Master"

Setting: Garden bench at sunset

(Inspired by verse 34 – Learn through humility, questioning, and service)

Aryan:
"Grandpa, if we can read books, why do we need a teacher?"

Grandpa Ved:
"Books show the path. But only a teacher can help you *walk* it."

Maya:
"And you... you were our secret teacher all along."

Grandpa Ved (smiling):
"Every child needs a little spark. Then the fire of wisdom burns on its own."

Final Scene: "The Real Victory"

Setting: Assembly Hall – Project Presentation

(Inspired by verses 35–42 – Knowledge removes doubt and brings peace)

Narration:
As the students share their project, Aryan sees a vision of the **Timekeeper**, who nods and vanishes. The doubt in Aryan's heart is gone. He now knows that actions, when done with understanding and purpose, become divine.

Moral of the Story:

True knowledge burns away confusion and guides action.
A wise teacher helps you discover your inner

strength.
Doing your duty selflessly is the highest form of wisdom.

Key Takeaways for Children:

- Wisdom is timeless and grows with sharing.
- Don't just do things—understand *why* you do them.
- Knowledge is like fire—it lights your way and burns your fear.
- Always respect and learn from wise teachers and elders.
- Giving your best with pure intention is a sacred offering.

Drama Attributes:

- **Genre:** Spiritual Drama with Fantasy Elements
- **Scenes:** 6 short, dramatic, dialogue-rich scenes
- **Tone:** Reflective, inspirational, curious
- **Props:** Garden bench, science fair setup, fire simulator, books

- **Symbolic Elements:** Timekeeper, Fire of Knowledge, Maze of Paths

Chapter 5

Title5: "The Peaceful Player: Aryan's Inner Game"

Characters:

- **Aryan** – A thoughtful 13-year-old student (Arjuna)
- **Grandpa Veer** – His wise mentor (Krishna)
- **Coach Shanti** – PE teacher who believes in peace through sports
- **Rohan** – Aryan's aggressive teammate
- **Priya** – A calm, silent observer (Symbol of inner renunciation)
- **The Mirror of Mind** – A magical mirror that reflects one's thoughts

Scene 1: The Big Game – Action vs Renunciation (Verse 5.1–5.2)

(The school organizes a football match. Aryan is chosen as the team leader. But he hesitates.)

Aryan (thinking): “Should I just sit out and watch? Games bring fights and ego…”

(Coach Shanti overhears.)

Coach Shanti:
"Renouncing the game isn’t peace, Aryan. True peace comes when you play, but without selfishness."

Grandpa Veer (entering with a whistle):
"Renunciation of action and doing your duty without ego both lead to the same truth. But action with detachment is superior."

Scene 2: The Calm Player in Chaos (Verse 5.7)

(During the game, Rohan is angry and aggressive. Aryan plays with focus but is peaceful, even when fouled.)

Rohan (yelling): "Why don’t you fight back, Aryan?"

Aryan (smiling):
"Because I’m playing the game—not the opponent."

Grandpa Veer (nodding):
"One who controls body and mind, who is

detached from results, is never touched by action—like a lotus untouched by muddy water."

Scene 3: Seeing All as Equal (Verse 5.18)

(After the game, Rohan mocks a substitute player from another class. Aryan steps in.)

Aryan:
"Every player on the field has a role—whether fast or slow, tall or short."

Priya (quietly):
"And every soul is equal in the eyes of wisdom."

Grandpa Veer:
"Whether a scholar, a servant, or a street kid, the wise see all beings as equal light in different lamps."

Scene 4: The Mirror of Mind (Verse 5.20)

(Aryan is shown a magical Mirror of Mind by Grandpa Veer.)

Mirror: *(glowing)*
"Let's see how you react to victory and failure."

(In one side of the mirror, Aryan is shown jumping with pride. On the other, sad and angry in defeat.)

Aryan:
"That's not me… is it?"

Grandpa Veer:
"Those who are not elated by success nor crushed by failure, who remain balanced—have truly found peace."

Scene 5: Freedom through Detachment (Verse 5.26–5.29)

(After the match, Aryan goes to a quiet corner and watches birds fly.)

Aryan (to Grandpa):
"I used to think peace meant sitting quietly. But now I see—it's being free *inside*, even while acting."

Grandpa Veer:
"Exactly. True peace is not escape. It's freedom from anger, desire, and ego. That is the blissful space within."

(The sun sets. Aryan, calm and smiling, walks back as the world buzzes around him.)

Moral of the Story:

"Peace doesn't mean stopping action—it means acting without ego, staying balanced in all situations, and seeing unity in all beings."

Allegory Table:

Verse	Teaching	Story Element
5.1–5.2	Action with detachment is better than inaction	Aryan choosing to play with detachment
5.7	Peace comes through self-control and detachment	Aryan playing calmly amidst chaos
5.18	Wisdom sees all beings as equal	Aryan defending a younger, mocked player
5.20	Stay balanced in joy and sorrow	Aryan sees the Mirror of Mind and reflects
5.26–5.29	Inner peace comes from freedom, not inactivity	Aryan realizes freedom is internal, not external rest

Chapter 5

Title5a: "The Bridge Between Doing and Letting Go"

Characters:

- **Aryan** – 13-year-old curious boy (represents Arjuna)
- **Grandpa Ved** – Wise, calm, former scientist and philosopher (represents Krishna)
- **Maya** – Aryan's smart and practical friend
- **Mr. Sankalp** – A new guest speaker at school (a calm yogi-like character)
- **Ms. Shraddha** – Teacher guiding them on inner peace and conflict
- **Mirror of Mind** – Symbolic figure in a dream representing clarity and reflection

Theme:

Explores the difference between **renunciation (sanyasa)** and **selfless action (karma yoga)**. True peace lies not in escaping the world but acting without attachment. Inner calmness, equality of vision, and detachment from results are highlighted.

Scene 1: "To Do or Not to Do?"
Setting: School Debate Hall
(Inspired by verses 1–6: Arjuna asks which path is better—action or renunciation)
Maya (arguing):
"If you want peace, just quit the race. Stop running behind success!"
Aryan:
"No way! What about responsibilities? You can't just sit back and watch."
Ms. Shraddha:
"Tomorrow, a guest will help you decide which is better: *Doing or Letting Go.*"

Scene 2: "The Guest Who Sees Both Sides"
Setting: Classroom with Mr. Sankalp's talk
(Inspired by verses 7–10: The enlightened person acts, but is unattached)
Mr. Sankalp (calmly):
"The wise neither escape work nor cling to it. They act, but they are free."
Aryan:
"So, you're saying doing work and giving it up… are both okay?"
Mr. Sankalp:
"Both lead to the same mountain peak—one walks, the other climbs. But without ego, action becomes meditation."

Maya:
"So karma yoga is like... being in the world but not owned by it?"
Mr. Sankalp (smiling):
"Exactly. Like a lotus in muddy water—it blooms untouched."

Scene 3: "Dream of the Mirror"
Setting: Aryan's dream world – mystical forest and a glowing mirror
(Inspired by verses 11–18: Seeing everyone equally, reflecting pure consciousness)
Narration:
Aryan dreams of the **Mirror of Mind**, which shows different faces—friend, enemy, rich, poor—all reflecting the same light.
Mirror:
"When you look with ego, you see separation. When you look with wisdom, all are one."
Aryan:
"So the wise see no difference between a priest and a beggar?"
Mirror:
"They see the *light within*, not the clothes outside."

Scene 4: "The Heat and the Fan"
Setting: Grandpa Ved's workshop – electric circuits and machines
(Inspired by verses 19–23: Freedom from desire brings inner joy)

Grandpa Ved:
"Desire is like heat. The more you want, the hotter it gets. Peace is like a fan—you cool down by letting go."
Aryan:
"But I feel proud when I win, and upset when I lose."
Grandpa Ved:
"That's natural. But a yogi feels happiness not from outcomes, but from the doing. That's lasting joy."
Maya:
"Like loving the game, not just the trophy?"
Grandpa Ved:
"Exactly."

Scene 5: "The Eye of Equality"
Setting: Playground – A match between mixed teams of students
(Inspired by verses 24–29: The one who sees God in all, sees truly)
Narration:
Aryan, once judgmental, now chooses players not by skill but spirit. He gives the chance to quiet kids, and they surprise everyone with teamwork.
Principal:
"Your team spirit is remarkable."
Aryan:
"I just saw their strengths, not their labels."
Mr. Sankalp (nodding):
"Now you're living *karma yoga*."

Moral of the Story:

Real peace comes not by quitting life but by living it without ego.
The wise act with full heart, yet stay free from the results.
True equality is seeing the same divine in all beings.

Key Takeaways for Children:

- You don't have to give up your duties to be peaceful—do them without fear or greed.
- Success and failure come and go—stay balanced through both.
- Karma Yoga = Action + Detachment = Peace.
- See all people equally—no one is higher or lower inside.
- Love the process, not just the reward.

Drama Attributes:

- **Genre:** Moral Drama with Spiritual Symbolism
- **Scenes:** 5 immersive scenes
- **Props:** Dream mirror, electric fans, workshop tools, sports equipment
- **Symbolism:** Mirror of Mind (equality), Lotus (detachment), Fan (cooling desires)
- **Mood:** Reflective, playful, inspiring

BHAGAVAD GITA
CHAPTER 5

Krishna symbolizes the inner divine guide, teaching the essence of renunciation through action. Arjuna represents the questioning mind, gradually awakening to inner stillness.

Chapter 6

Title6: "The Inner Champion: Aryan's Quiet Power"

Main Characters:

- **Aryan** – A curious 13-year-old student (Arjuna)
- **Grandpa Veer** – The wise mentor (Krishna)
- **Coach Shanti** – Sports teacher and silent guide
- **Riya** – A talkative friend who struggles to focus
- **Maya** – A silent, disciplined artist
- **The Inner Room** – A magical room representing the mind

Scene 1: "The New Competition" (Verse 6.1–6.2)

(Aryan is invited to a new school event: the "Mind Challenge." It's not a game of strength, but of silence, focus, and discipline.)

Riya:
"Ugh, no gadgets, no talking? This is impossible!"

Aryan (puzzled):
"But how can *doing nothing* be winning?"

Coach Shanti (smiling):
"A true yogi is one who does his duties without attachment to rewards. Renunciation isn't laziness—it's disciplined action done in silence."

Scene 2: "The Inner Room" (Verse 6.5–6.6)

(Aryan is led to a special room called the "Inner Room." It has no distractions—just a mat and a mirror.)

Grandpa Veer (appearing magically):
"Aryan, your best friend or worst enemy is not someone outside. It's *your own mind*. Lift yourself with your thoughts. Don't let them pull you down."

Mirror of the Mind (glowing):
"See what you think—you become what you focus on."

Scene 3: "Balanced Like a Candle" (Verse 6.8–6.9)

(Aryan sees Maya, the silent artist, painting without reacting to praise or teasing.)

Aryan (watching):
"She doesn't even flinch. How?"

Grandpa Veer:
"The wise are equal to friend, foe, or critic. Like a candle in still air—they glow steady. That's true balance."

Scene 4: "Learning to Sit Still" (Verse 6.10–6.13)

(Aryan is told to meditate every morning at the same time, in the same place. The first few days, he struggles—scratching, thinking of lunch, etc.)

Aryan:
"This is harder than math!"

Grandpa Veer (laughing gently):
"Even great warriors must train their minds. Sit straight. Breathe. Close your eyes. Make your *seat firm*, and let your thoughts slow down."

(A calming flute sound plays. Slowly, Aryan begins to settle.)

Scene 5: "Like a Steady Flame" (Verse 6.19)

(After a week, Aryan sits calmly in the Inner Room. The wind howls outside, but he doesn't move.)

Grandpa Veer (appearing):
"When your mind is steady like a lamp in a windless room—you are meditating."

Scene 6: "The Slip and the Climb" (Verse 6.37–6.40)

(Aryan misses his meditation one day, plays games instead, and feels guilty.)

Aryan:
"I failed. I can't be a yogi."

Grandpa Veer:
"No effort is wasted, Aryan. Even a little practice protects you. Falling isn't failing—quitting is."

(The mirror flashes a scene of Aryan lifting a fallen child during a race. He understands.)

Scene 7: "The Greatest Yogi" (Verse 6.46–6.47)

(In the final round of the Mind Challenge, others chant, some show off poses, but Aryan simply sits... smiling, quiet, focused.)

Coach Shanti:
"The highest yogi isn't the most flexible. It's the

one with love, balance, and steady mind—like Aryan."

Grandpa Veer (smiling in the background): "And the greatest of yogis is the one who loves and remembers Me with full heart. That is true meditation."

Moral of the Story:

"Meditation is not running away from life—but training your mind to stay steady in all of life's moments. The true champion is not the loudest, but the calmest within."

Allegory Table:

Verse	Teaching	Story Element
6.1–6.2	True renunciation is doing duty without desire	Aryan joins the Mind Challenge with discipline
6.5–6.6	Uplift yourself through your own mind	Aryan meets the Mirror of Mind in the Inner Room
6.8–6.9	Equal vision towards friend, enemy, critic	Maya the artist

		ignores praise and insult
6.10–6.13	Meditate in a clean, quiet space with firm posture	Aryan struggles and learns proper meditation
6.19	Mind steady like a lamp in still air	Aryan reaches calmness in the Inner Room
6.37–6.40	No effort is wasted; even failure leads forward	Aryan skips one day but keeps trying
6.46–6.47	The greatest yogi loves and connects with God	Aryan meditates with love, not just silence

Chapter 6

Title6a: "The Sky Within: The Journey of Young Yogi Yash"

Main Characters:

- **Yash** – A playful but thoughtful 12-year-old boy (symbolizes Arjuna)
- **Grandpa Hari** – A wise and calm retired forest ranger, Yash's mentor (symbolizes Krishna)
- **Maya** – Yash's energetic best friend (symbolizes restlessness of the mind)
- **Yogi Robo** – A talking robot yoga instructor (comic relief + discipline figure)
- **Inner Sky** – Allegory for the peaceful, meditative self
- **Stormy Thoughts** – Represents distractions and worldly temptations

Chapter Theme:

The path of meditation, self-discipline, balance, and the greatness of a true yogi who finds peace within.

Scene 1: "No More Video Games?!?"

(Inspired by Verses 6.1–6.2)

(Yash is playing video games for hours. Grandpa Hari walks in.)

Grandpa Hari (softly):
"Yash, a true master doesn't just escape work. He works with focus and detachment."

Yash:
"But Grandpa! Games are fun! Meditation is boring."

Grandpa Hari:
"Do you want real power? A yogi controls his mind, not the other way around. Let's take a challenge—7 days to become a Sky Explorer!"

Yash (excited):
"Like a Jedi?! I'm in!"

Scene 2: "Meet Yogi Robo"

(Inspired by Verses 6.3–6.4)

(They enter a wooden cabin in the backyard. A yoga robot named Yogi Robo boots up.)

Yogi Robo:
"Namaste, young seeker. Detachment mode activated. Begin self-mastery level one."

Yash (giggling):
"He talks like Grandpa!"

Grandpa Hari:
"He *is* my meditation partner. He'll teach you how to rise above likes and dislikes."

Scene 3: "Balance is the Key!"

(Inspired by Verses 6.5–6.9)

(Yash tries meditating but falls asleep.)

Yogi Robo:
"ERROR! You cannot lift your mind if you let it sleep."

Grandpa Hari:
"A balanced life is the yogi's path. Not too much food, sleep, or play. Control your body, then the mind follows."

Yash:
"Okay! I'll eat less ice cream and sleep on time!"

Scene 4: "The Inner Sky"

(Inspired by Verses 6.10–6.17)

(Yash sits under a tree, eyes closed. Inside his mind, he enters the "Sky Within." Stars twinkle. But suddenly...)

Stormy Thoughts (loud):
"Hey! You forgot your math test! Your friend called you a slow runner!"

Yash (scared):
"I can't concentrate! My mind is yelling!"

Grandpa Hari (voice echoes):
"Steady… like a candle in a windless room. Let the storm pass."

Yash breathes deeply. The sky clears. Silence fills his mind.

Scene 5: "I Found Me!"

(Inspired by Verses 6.18–6.23)

Yash (smiling):
"Grandpa! I was… floating in peace. No thoughts. Just… me. Is that meditation?"

Grandpa Hari:
"Yes, child. When the mind is quiet, you see your real self. That joy never fades."

Scene 6: "But I Lost It Again!"

(Inspired by Verses 6.24–6.26)

(The next day, Yash tries to meditate but gets distracted by a phone buzz.)

Yash (groaning):
"I lost it! My Inner Sky disappeared!"

Yogi Robo:
"Reboot required. Gently bring the mind back. Again and again."

Grandpa Hari:
"Even the greatest yogis slip. What matters is not giving up."

Scene 7: "A Little Goes a Long Way"

(Inspired by Verses 6.27–6.32)

(Yash helps Maya with her homework instead of playing.)

Maya:
"You're becoming so kind! What happened to the old Yash?"

Yash (grinning):
"I found peace by thinking of others. Meditation doesn't end on the mat."

Scene 8: "What if I Fail?"

(Inspired by Verses 6.37–6.40)

Yash (worried):
"Grandpa, what if I can't stay focused forever?"

Grandpa Hari:
"Don't worry, Yash. Every good effort stays with

you—even after this life. One who walks the yogi's path never truly fails."

Scene 9: "The Supreme Yogi"

(Inspired by Verses 6.46–6.47)

Yogi Robo:
"Analysis complete. Yash shows signs of becoming the highest Yogi."

Yash (surprised):
"Me? I'm not even perfect!"

Grandpa Hari:
"You love God with your whole heart. That makes you the best yogi. Not power, not poses—just pure love."

Final Scene: "The Sky Belongs to All"

(Yash writes in his journal)

"In the Inner Sky, there's no fear, no anger. Just peace. I can always return there—if I listen, breathe, and love."

Moral of the Story:

"True peace comes not from the outside world, but from balancing your mind, loving all, and connecting to the peace within. A yogi is one who keeps trying, one breath at a time."

Allegory Table:

Verse Set	Theme	Story Allegory
6.1–6.2	Detachment and true renunciation	Yash gives up games for higher learning
6.3–6.4	Self-discipline	Yogi Robo trains Yash
6.5–6.9	Mind is friend/enemy	Yash controls cravings & moods
6.10–6.17	Meditative lifestyle	Entering "Inner Sky" amid mental storms
6.18–6.23	Bliss of meditation	Deep peace without thoughts
6.24–6.26	Patience in practice	Yash brings mind back after distraction
6.27–6.32	Yogi sees all beings as equal	Yash helps Maya, shows compassion
6.37–6.40	No effort is wasted	Yash's doubts and Grandpa's encouragement
6.46–6.47	Highest yogi loves God	Yash's love and discipline make him the best

Chapter 7

Title7: "The Secret Behind Everything: Aryan's Science Fair Discovery"

Main Characters:

- **Aryan** – The curious 13-year-old student (Arjuna)
- **Grandpa Veer** – Wise guide (Krishna)
- **Anaya** – A science genius and classmate
- **Mr. Cosmos** – The school principal (Represents Supreme Knowledge)
- **Aryan's Inner Voice** – Symbolizes conscience and God within
- **Science Fair Models** – Represent nature's elements and divine powers

Scene 1: The Science Fair Announcement (Verse 7.1–7.2)

(School announces an interschool science fair. Aryan is excited but confused on what topic to pick.)

Aryan:
"Should I make a robot? A volcano? A water purifier?"

Grandpa Veer:
"This time, choose something deeper—discover the hidden force behind all of life."

Aryan:
"Hidden force? Like... magic?"

Grandpa Veer (smiling):
"Not magic—*Me*. Know Me fully—with both knowledge (*jnana*) and wisdom (*vijnana*). Then you'll see the truth behind all things."

Scene 2: The 8 Powers of Nature (Verse 7.4–7.5)

(Aryan creates 8 science fair models: earth, water, fire, air, space, mind, intellect, and ego. Anaya watches, impressed.)

Anaya:
"These are just science models…"

Aryan:
"But together, they form nature! And the life in us—that's a higher power. Grandpa says it's like God is the battery behind everything!"

Scene 3: Strings of a Puppet Show (Verse 7.7)

(Aryan watches a puppet show. The puppets dance—but the strings are hidden.)

Grandpa Veer (appearing):
"I am the string behind all living beings. Everything is strung on Me like pearls on a thread."

Aryan (gasps):
"So… nothing moves on its own?"

Grandpa:
"Everything you see is connected to Me—even if it looks separate."

Scene 4: Many Faces, One Source (Verse 7.8–7.9)

(At the fair, people enjoy fruit juice, firecrackers, cool breeze, and water spray. Aryan explains each.)

Aryan (demonstrating):
"The sweetness in fruits? That's Him. The heat in fire? That's Him. The life in breath? That's also Him."

Anaya (whispering):
"So, He's in *everything*?"

Aryan (nodding):
"Yes—even in your favorite mango lassi."

Scene 5: Why People Don't See the Truth (Verse 7.13–7.15)

(Aryan notices many booths focusing only on winning, money, or fame. Some kids even mock his exhibit.)

Aryan:
"Why don't they understand the bigger truth?"

Grandpa Veer:
"Because they're trapped by three powers—desire, anger, and confusion. These cover their vision like clouds over the sun."

Scene 6: The Four Seekers (Verse 7.16–7.18)

(Visitors come to Aryan's booth for different reasons.)

- A girl asks: "Can this help me win?"
- A boy says: "I want peace in my mind."
- Another says: "I love learning new things."
- And one quietly smiles and says: "I feel something divine in this."

Grandpa Veer (to Aryan):
"There are four types of seekers—those in trouble, those who want things, those who seek knowledge, and those who love Me. The last one is the best—they seek Me for Me alone."

Scene 7: The Puzzle of Life (Verse 7.19)

(Aryan builds a 1,000-piece puzzle showing a glowing Earth. The last piece is a symbol of God at the center.)

Anaya:
"So, after all learning, the real truth is… God is behind everything?"

Aryan (placing the final piece):
"Yes. After many births, the wise person sees this and says, 'Everything is God'. That's true wisdom."

Moral of the Story:

"Real knowledge is not just knowing the parts of the world, but understanding the One who connects them all. He is the sweetness in fruit, the warmth in the sun, the breath in us, and the wisdom behind all wonders."

Allegory Table:

Verse	Teaching	Scene/Story Element
7.1–7.2	Know Me completely with knowledge and wisdom	Aryan chooses a deeper science topic
7.4–7.5	Nature is made of 8 elements, plus the higher living force	Aryan's 8-element science models
7.7	All beings are strung in Me like pearls on a thread	Puppet show metaphor
7.8–7.9	God is in taste, heat, air, water, and life	Aryan explains common elements as symbols of God
7.13–7.15	People are deluded by nature's 3 modes	Some students focus on fame, greed, and fun
7.16–7.18	Four types of seekers, the wise devotee is the highest	Visitors to Aryan's booth with different mindsets
7.19	True wisdom: Everything is God	Puzzle completed with divine center

Chapter 7

Title7a: "The Invisible Wi-Fi: Discovering the Hidden Connection"

Main Characters:

- **Aarav** – Curious 12-year-old boy, symbolizing Arjuna
- **Grandma Meera** – Wise and gentle, symbolizing Krishna
- **Riya** – Aarav's tech-savvy friend
- **Invisible Wi-Fi Signal** – Metaphor for God's presence
- **App World** – Symbol for material nature
- **Virus Bug** – Symbol for Maya (illusion)

Theme:

Understanding how the Divine is the essence of everything, beyond forms, and how true wisdom leads us beyond illusions like Maya.

Scene 1: "Grandma, What Powers Everything?"

(Inspired by Verse 7.1–7.3)

(Aarav and Riya sit with their devices at Grandma Meera's house, frustrated due to slow internet.)

Aarav:
"Why isn't anything loading? My app shows full battery but no internet!"

Grandma Meera (smiling):
"That's because the real power—the Wi-Fi—is invisible. The phone has all features but can't work without that signal. Just like your body and brain can't work without the Divine spark within you."

Riya (curious):
"So God is like... an invisible Wi-Fi?"

Grandma Meera:
"Yes! You can't see Him, but He powers everything. To connect, you need the password of devotion and wisdom."

Scene 2: "The Elements and the Signal"

(Inspired by Verses 7.4–7.6)

(Grandma shows them a science kit with Earth, Water, Fire, Air, Ether, Mind, Intellect, and Ego models.)

Grandma Meera:
"These are like layers of the app world—your body and senses. But who created and connects all these? The One Signal—the Divine Consciousness."

Aarav:
"So even my thoughts and feelings are like apps powered by the same signal?"

Grandma:
"Exactly! The Divine is both the hardware and the hidden energy behind everything."

Scene 3: "The Trick of Maya the Bug"

(Inspired by Verses 7.13–7.15)

(Suddenly, Riya's screen goes blank. A cartoonish "Virus Bug" appears on screen.)

Virus Bug (laughing):
"Ha! You thought everything was running fine. I trick you to forget the real source. Look at the shiny apps and ignore the signal!"

Grandma Meera:
"That's Maya—illusion. It makes you think

temporary things are permanent and hides the truth. Only devotion and clear understanding can remove it."

Scene 4: "Signal is in Everything!"

(Inspired by Verses 7.8–7.12)

(Aarav steps outside and looks at nature—flowers, sun, rain, birds.)

Aarav (thinking):
"The signal is everywhere—in sunlight, the cool breeze, the strength of the mountains, the taste of water..."

Grandma Meera:
"You got it! The Divine is the beauty in beauty, the intelligence in intellect, the strength in strength."

Scene 5: "Four Users, Four Logins"

(Inspired by Verses 7.16–7.19)

(They watch a cartoon video showing four types of users logging in to the Divine Signal:)

1. **Seeker 1 – Wants help in trouble**
2. **Seeker 2 – Wants something worldly**
3. **Seeker 3 – Is curious**

4. **Seeker 4 – Loves the Divine just for who He is**

Riya:
"Which is the best user, Grandma?"

Grandma Meera:
"The one who connects out of pure love and wisdom. But all users are welcome—God accepts all!"

Scene 6: "Many Apps, One Source"

(Inspired by Verses 7.20–7.23)

(Kids see people using different apps for video, music, chatting… but all using the same Wi-Fi.)

Aarav:
"So people worship different forms, but all are trying to reach the same Source?"

Grandma Meera:
"Yes, but not all reach the full truth. Forms are helpful, but wisdom reveals the formless, infinite Divine behind all."

Scene 7: "Rare Connection"

(Inspired by Verse 7.3 & 7.19)

(A screen pops up: 'Only 1 in millions truly knows Me completely.')

Aarav:
"Why so rare?"

Grandma Meera:
"Because most users forget the Source and get lost in the apps. But a rare soul sees through the illusion and connects directly to the Signal with love and awareness."

Final Scene: "The Ultimate Connection"

(Aarav writes in his journal)

"God is not far. He's the power in everything. If I remember Him, I stay connected—even when the screen goes dark."

Grandma Meera (smiling):
"You've learned the true Wi-Fi secret, my child."

Moral of the Story:

"The Divine is the invisible power that runs everything. Remembering Him with love and wisdom helps us stay connected, even when life gets confusing."

Allegory Table:

Verse	Theme	Story Element
7.1–7.3	Importance of devotion & wisdom	Grandma explains Wi-Fi and

		password metaphor
7.4–7.6	Divine is source of all material & mind	Science kit with 8 elements and the hidden Signal
7.8–7.12	God in all experiences and qualities	Nature walk and discovering Divine in all senses
7.13–7.15	Maya traps beings in illusion	Virus Bug distracts from true source
7.16–7.19	Four kinds of devotees	Cartoon of four user types
7.20–7.23	People worship various forms	Different apps connected to same Wi-Fi
7.3 & 7.19	Rare soul knows the Supreme	Message: 1 in millions connects truly

Chapter 8

Title8: "The Skyward Journey: Aryan and the Rocket of Thought"

Main Characters:

- **Aryan** – The curious student (Arjuna)
- **Grandpa Veer** – The wise guide (Krishna)
- **Rhea** – A science enthusiast and Aryan's best friend
- **Principal Cosmos** – Represents divine knowledge
- **Captain Astro** – Space pilot (represents the inner self)
- **The Rocket** – Metaphor for the body and journey of the soul

Scene 1: "Questions in the Night" (Verse 8.1–8.3)

(Aryan lies on the terrace under the stars, talking to Grandpa Veer)

Aryan:
"Grandpa, what is the soul? What is God? Where do we go after we die? And what is karma?"

Grandpa Veer (smiling):
"All great questions, Aryan. The soul (*Adhyatma*) is your true self. God (*Brahman*) is the Supreme, and karma is your action's energy. When we understand these, life becomes clear."

Scene 2: "The Rocket Blueprint" (Verse 8.4–8.6)

(Aryan and Rhea plan a model rocket for a school contest.)

Rhea:
"What if our rocket loses direction at the last minute?"

Grandpa Veer (overhearing):
"Just like a rocket flies toward where it's aimed, the soul also travels at death in the direction of its final thoughts. Always keep your mind focused on the Divine."

Scene 3: "Captain Astro's Mission" (Verse 8.7–8.8)

*(Inside Aryan's imagination, he becomes **Captain Astro**, flying a spaceship.)*

Control Center (voice of Grandpa):
"Captain Astro, repeat this during your mission: 'I serve the Supreme. My focus is clear. My goal is light.'"

Captain Astro:
"I understand! I must remember Him at all times—even during action."

(Verse 8.7 teaches practice of remembering God while acting. Verse 8.8 highlights meditation and focus on the Divine at death.)

Scene 4: "The Light Beyond the Sky" (Verse 8.9–8.10)

(Captain Astro sees a beautiful golden star far beyond the galaxies.)

Captain Astro (in awe):
"That must be the Imperishable Light—beyond darkness and time!"

Grandpa Veer (as voiceover):
"That's Him—pure, eternal, radiant like the sun. Those who remember Him in their last moment, with a steady mind, reach Him forever."

Scene 5: "The Eternal Pathways" (Verse 8.23–8.26)

(Back in school, Aryan builds two space paths—one glowing with light, one fading into darkness.)

Aryan (explaining to the judges):
"Some souls travel the **path of light**, never to return, reaching the Supreme. Others take the **path of darkness**, and return for another chance to learn."

Rhea:
"So the way we live and think really affects where we go?"

Aryan:
"Exactly! Our focus, love, and truth shape our soul's journey."

Scene 6: "The Real Launch" (Verse 8.27–8.28)

(The science fair ends. Aryan gazes at the stars again.)

Grandpa Veer:
"Know this, Aryan—whoever understands these paths and lives with devotion rises above karma, rituals, and fears. They live in freedom, like the rocket that reaches the stars and never crashes back."

Moral of the Story:

"What you constantly think of becomes your destination. Live with purpose, remember the higher truth, and you'll soar beyond limits like a rocket headed for the stars."

Allegory Table:

Verse	Concept	Story Element
8.1–8.3	Questions about soul, God, karma	Aryan's questions under the stars
8.4–8.6	Last thought shapes the soul's path	Rocket must be aimed right; last moment focus
8.7–8.8	Remembrance of God during action and death	Captain Astro repeats Divine mission focus
8.9–8.10	Focused mind sees the Supreme radiant form	Astro sees the Golden Light beyond galaxies
8.23–8.26	Two paths after death – light (no return), dark (return)	Two rocket paths: luminous and fading
8.27–8.28	Knowing this gives freedom beyond karma	Aryan understands spiritual freedom is the highest science

Chapter 8

Title8a: "The Final Flight: Aryan and the Rocket of Remembrance"

Main Characters:

- **Aryan** – A 12-year-old boy, thoughtful and curious (symbolizing Arjuna)
- **Grandpa Veer** – A wise storyteller and Aryan's grandfather (symbolizing Krishna)
- **Rhea** – Aryan's friend and science partner
- **Captain Astro** – Imaginative superhero representing the soul
- **The Rocket** – Symbol of the human body
- **The Galaxy of Light** – Symbolizes the Supreme (Brahman)

- **Shadow Path** – Symbol of the path of ignorance

Scene 1: "What Lies Beyond the Sky?"

(Inspired by Verses 8.1–8.3)

(Evening. Aryan sits on the terrace, looking at stars. Grandpa Veer joins him.)

Aryan (pointing at the sky):
"Grandpa, what happens after death? Where do we go? What is this soul you always talk about?"

Grandpa Veer (smiling):
"Ah, these are questions even kings and sages have asked! Let me explain: The *soul* is the real you, beyond your body. *Brahman* is the Supreme, everywhere and in everything. Your *karma* is the energy of all your actions. These decide your path."

Scene 2: "Rocket Mission: Last Thought"

(Inspired by Verses 8.4–8.6)

(In Aryan's imagination, he and Rhea build a rocket. They name it 'Soulcraft-1'. The final destination depends on the last code entered before launch.)

Rhea:
"So if we press the right code at launch, the rocket goes to the Galaxy of Light?"

Grandpa Veer (voice-over):
"Just like this rocket, where your mind is at the final moment of life decides where your soul goes. If you remember the Divine at the end, you reach Him."

Scene 3: "Meditation Mode Activated"

(Inspired by Verses 8.7–8.8)

(Captain Astro prepares to launch Soulcraft-1. He chants a mantra.)

Captain Astro:
"My focus is only on the One. My thoughts are clear. I remember Him always, in everything I do!"

Grandpa Veer (voiceover):
"Practice remembering the Divine in all actions. When your last thought is on the Supreme, you travel to Him."

Scene 4: "The Light Beyond All Lights"

(Inspired by Verses 8.9–8.10)

(The rocket crosses planets and stars. Suddenly, they see a glowing sphere brighter than a thousand suns.)

Aryan (as Captain Astro):
“That must be the Source! It’s bright… yet peaceful.”

Grandpa Veer (narrating):
“The one who focuses their life on this eternal Light—the formless, endless, timeless Being—reaches the ultimate destination.”

Scene 5: “Path of Light and Path of Shadows”

(Inspired by Verses 8.23–8.26)

(Aryan dreams of two roads from Earth: one made of golden starlight, one dark and foggy.)

Captain Astro:
"Which path should I take?"

A Divine Voice:
“The path of Light leads to freedom—you don’t return. The dark path leads you back to Earth. Choose with clarity.”

Aryan (waking up):
"Now I get it! Our deeds, thoughts, and focus decide our future path."

Scene 6: "Graduation from the School of Life"

(Inspired by Verses 8.27–8.28)

(At school, Aryan presents the project 'Soulcraft Journey' at the science fair.)

Aryan (to the audience):
"If you know how to aim your mind and heart toward something greater, you won't be confused. You rise above karma. Even beyond rituals and rules, it's your love and remembrance of the Higher that matters most."

Principal Cosmos (clapping):
"You've captured the spirit of both science and soul!"

Moral of the Story:

"Your last thought shapes your soul's flight. Live every day with awareness, purpose, and connection to the Higher. Then, when it's time to launch, you'll rise toward the Light."

Allegory table:

Verse	Theme	Story Element
8.1–8.3	Soul, God, Karma	Aryan asks Grandpa Veer about life and death
8.4–8.6	Final thought decides rebirth	Rocket mission depends on last launch code
8.7–8.8	Constant remembrance of God	Captain Astro chants and stays focused
8.9–8.10	Meditate on the Eternal	Soulcraft-1 sees the Galaxy of Light
8.23–8.26	Path of Light vs. Path of Darkness	Two paths after death shown in Aryan's dream
8.27–8.28	Freedom through wisdom and devotion	Aryan's presentation at the science fair

Chapter 9

Title9: "The Secret Within the Heart: Aryan's Royal Discovery"

Main Characters:

- **Aryan** – The curious 12-year-old boy from earlier stories
- **Grandma Gita** – A wise grandmother figure who reveals deep truths through stories (like Krishna)
- **Vikram** – Aryan's best friend who loves science and proof
- **The Invisible King** – A magical king who lives in every heart (represents Krishna)
- **Heart Castle** – A mystical place where the Invisible King rules

Central Theme:

The greatest secret is that God lives in every heart. He loves everyone equally and those who remember Him with love are never lost.

Scene 1: "The Royal Secret Begins"

(Based on Verse 9.1–2)

(Aryan visits Grandma, looking puzzled with a paper titled: "Secrets of the Universe")

Aryan:
"Grandma, why do some kids always win, while others try so hard but don't? Isn't there a secret way to succeed?"

Grandma Gita (smiling):
"Yes, my dear. There is a royal secret, the most sacred knowledge, and you're ready for it."

(The room glows and shifts to a dreamy space—the Heart Castle appears.)

Scene 2: "The Heart Castle & The Invisible King"

(Verse 9.3–4)

(They enter a magical castle inside Aryan's own chest.)

Narrator:
"This is the Heart Castle. The Invisible King lives here, in you and everyone."

Aryan:
"But where is He? I don't see Him!"

Grandma:
"He is in all, yet not seen. Like air fills every space but can't be caught."

Scene 3: "The Fire that Eats Without Eating"

(Verse 9.5–6)

(Aryan watches a fire eat a paper, but the paper turns to light instead of ash.)

Grandma:
"God works like this fire—He takes care of all without taking anything for Himself."

Aryan:
"Wow… so He does everything but wants nothing?"

Scene 4: "The Wheel That Turns On Its Own"

(Verse 9.7–10)

(A spinning golden wheel appears, creating seasons and life)

Grandma:
"Time, nature, creation—all move in cycles. God turns the wheel, but lets it spin on its own."

Aryan (in awe):
"He's the hidden mover of the world!"

Scene 5: "Why People Forget the King"

(Verse 9.11–12)

Vikram enters, laughing.

Vikram:
"An invisible king? Ha! I only believe what I can see and test!"

Grandma:
"Many mock the divine because He looks ordinary. But those who mock miss the magic."

Aryan:
"He may seem like us, but He is the source of everything?"

Scene 6: "The Devoted Scientist"

(Verse 9.13–14)

(Aryan imagines a scientist praying before starting experiments.)

Narrator:
"True wisdom is using knowledge to praise the Creator of all knowledge."

Aryan:
"Being smart and being devoted can go together!"

Scene 7: "God Accepts All Offerings with Love"

(Verse 9.22–26)

(Aryan watches a little girl offer a flower to an empty swing, smiling.)

Grandma:
"She believes her friend God is sitting there. And He accepts her flower with love."

Aryan:
"So God doesn't need gold—just love?"

Grandma:
"Yes. A leaf, a flower, or a simple prayer, if given with love, reaches Him."

Scene 8: "No One Is Left Behind"

(Verse 9.29–31)

(They see an old man, a thief, and a teacher all glowing with the same light.)

Aryan:
"Even a thief?"

Grandma:
"If he turns with true love and changes his ways, God sees his heart—not his past."

Scene 9: "The Eternal Devotee"

(Verse 9.32–34)

(Aryan sees the Heart Castle again, where people from all walks of life pray together.)

Grandma:
"Anyone—boy or girl, rich or poor—can reach the King with love and surrender."

Aryan (teary-eyed):
"It's so simple! Just remember Him with love…"

Final Scene: "The Royal Secret is Love"

(Aryan sits to meditate. A glowing figure—the Invisible King—appears briefly in his heart.)

King:
"You found me, Aryan. I was always here."

Grandma Gita:

"Now you know the royal secret: God lives in every heart, waiting to be remembered with love."

Moral of the Story:

"The greatest secret is not hidden in the stars, but in your heart. God loves all equally. Those who remember Him with love, no matter who they are, will never be lost."

Allegory Table:

Verse Set	Gita Message	Story Allegory
9.1–2	Supreme knowledge, easy & joyful	Grandma opens Aryan's path to inner discovery
9.3–4	God is in all things	Heart Castle & Invisible King
9.5–6	God acts but remains detached	Fire that eats without eating
9.7–10	All nature cycles through God	Spinning Wheel of Life
9.11–12	People mock what they don't understand	Vikram's disbelief
9.13–14	Wise ones know and praise the Divine	Devoted Scientist

9.22–26	God accepts even a leaf if offered with love	Little girl's flower offering
9.29–31	God sees the heart, not the past	The thief's glow
9.32–34	Everyone can attain Him with love	The Heart Castle gathering

Chapter 9

Title9a: "The Secret Within: Aarav's Discovery"

Characters:

- **Aarav (Arjuna)** – Now more confident, still curious
- **Krish Sir (Krishna)** – His wise mentor
- **Sneha** – Aarav's younger sister who is deeply observant
- **Principal Vedaji** – A mysterious principal who symbolizes divine presence
- **Magic Science Club** – Represents seekers of truth
- **Invisible Helper "Isha"** – Symbol of the Divine in all

Scene 1: The Secret Nobody Sees (Verse 1–3)

Krish Sir (in the school library):
"Aarav, today I will tell you the **king of secrets**, known only to few. It's not hidden because it's complicated… it's hidden because people don't believe it!"

Aarav: "A secret? Like magic?"

Krish Sir: "Better than magic. It's the power that runs this entire school—and the whole universe!"

Allegory: The secret knowledge is like a school rule that keeps everything running—but invisible to most.

Scene 2: The Principal's Presence (Verse 4–10)

Sneha (whispers): "I've never seen Principal Vedaji, but I hear he watches everything."

Krish Sir (nods): "Yes, his presence is everywhere, though you can't see him. He doesn't interfere, but his *energy* keeps things flowing."

Aarav: "Like gravity? We don't see it, but it holds us!"

Allegory: The Divine is in everything but not attached. Like air, like gravity—everywhere, invisible, powerful.

Scene 3: Who Really Works? (Verse 9–12)

Krish Sir: "Vedaji doesn't need anything from the school. He gives, creates, maintains—but doesn't claim."

Aarav: "But people still don't believe in him. Some say he's fake!"

Krish Sir: "Yes, they use the system but don't trust its source. That's why they're always restless."

Allegory: People who ignore the inner presence lose peace. Disbelief disconnects them.

Scene 4: The Divine In All (Verse 13–19)

Scene: Magic Science Club meeting

Aarav (to Sneha): "Do you know the plants we grow need sun, water, and time—but they also grow when we care for them?"

Krish Sir (entering): "Exactly! The **Divine is like the sun**—nourishing all. He takes the form of time, rain, giver, and receiver."

Allegory: The Divine is the sun, the rain, the soil, and even the gardener.

Scene 5: Easy Devotion (Verse 20–26)

Sneha: "I thought big rituals and tough chants are needed to please God…"

Krish Sir: "No, my dear. Even if you offer a flower, a leaf, or water with love—it reaches Him."

Aarav: "So… it's about feeling, not fancy things!"

Allegory: Love is the real offering. Even a small act becomes divine when done with love.

Scene 6: Equal Love for All (Verse 27–34)

Aarav (to the class): "From now, every club member must serve—even those who made mistakes earlier."

Sneha: "Why?"

Aarav: "Because everyone deserves a chance. Even those who've gone wrong can change with true devotion."

Krish Sir (smiling): "You're becoming the king of secret knowledge, Aarav. You're seeing everyone as equals."

Allegory: God sees all equally. Devotion cleanses all faults.

Allegory Table:

Verse Range	Allegory/Story Element	Metaphor
9.1–3	Secret knowledge shared by Krish Sir	Hidden truth = not far, just unseen due to disbelief
9.4–10	Principal Vedaji's unseen presence	Divine pervades all but remains unattached
9.9–12	Non-believers mock system but suffer	Disconnected minds lose peace
9.13–19	Sun, water, time as symbols of Divine presence	God = cause, giver, energy, and outcome
9.20–26	Offering of flower, water by Sneha	Devotion > ritual
9.27–34	Aarav includes all students, even misbehaving ones	God accepts all who love sincerely

Kids' Insights & Takeaways

1. **The divine is everywhere** – Like air or Wi-Fi, you may not see it, but it's working.
2. **Simple acts of love matter** – Even a small kind act becomes big when done with the heart.

3. **Belief brings peace** – When you trust the system (or God), life feels guided.
4. **All are equal before the divine** – Mistakes don't define you; your love and actions do.
5. **True knowledge is about feeling the connection** – not just reading books.

Chapter 10

Title10: "The Treasure Map of Wonders"

Main Characters:

- **Aryan** – The curious 12-year-old boy
- **Grandma Gita** – The wise, storytelling grandmother (symbol of Krishna)
- **Maya** – Aryan's imaginative cousin
- **The Cosmic Guide** – A glowing figure who guides them (represents Krishna's universal form)
- **The Treasure Map** – A magical map leading to the "Divine Wonders"

Central Theme:

Everything great, powerful, beautiful, wise, or wonderful is a spark of the Divine. By seeing this, we feel awe, love, and connection to the Divine in all.

Scene 1: "The Glowing Map Appears"

(Verses 10.1–4)

(Aryan is playing a board game with Maya. He opens the box and finds a glowing, rolled-up scroll inside.)

Aryan (reading):
"To know the greatest secret of all... follow this map."

Maya:
"Is it a treasure map?!"

(They touch it. Whoosh! The room turns into a magical forest. A glowing figure appears.)

Cosmic Guide:
"I am the one who gave this knowledge long ago. Now I'll show you my glories!"

Scene 2: "I Am the Source of All"

(Verse 10.8–10)

(The Guide waves his hand. Aryan sees water flowing from a mountain, stars

bursting into life, and a seed growing into a tree.)

Cosmic Guide:
"I am the source of all things. The wise love Me and speak about Me with joy."

Maya:
"Everything begins from You?"

Guide:
"Yes, and those who truly seek Me, I light their path."

Scene 3: "Inside the Mind of the Divine"

(Verse 10.11)

(They enter a glowing brain-shaped cave with flashes of thoughts, ideas, and inventions.)

Guide:
"I destroy darkness with the lamp of knowledge. When someone sincerely seeks truth, I light their heart."

Scene 4: "I Am the Best of Everything"

(Verses 10.19–39)

(Now the treasure map opens fully. Each glowing symbol leads to a scene...)

1. “I am the Sun among lights”

(Aryan shields his eyes from a brilliant sun.)

Guide:
“When you see light, remember Me.”

2. “I am the thunderbolt among weapons”

(Maya watches a dragon spit a lightning bolt.)

Guide:
“In every mighty force, I am present.”

3. “I am Garuda among birds”

(A giant eagle soars above.)

Maya (excited):
“He’s majestic!”

Guide:
“In every graceful flight and power, I shine.”

4. “Among the wise, I am wisdom”

(A scientist in a lab explains the solar system.)

Aryan:
“Even intelligence is God’s spark?”

5. “Among trees, I am the sacred fig”

(A huge peepal tree glows softly.)

Guide:
“When you admire beauty or strength, remember: It’s Me.”

6. "I am the beginning, middle, and end of all"

(Sounds of a song playing – start, middle, ending.)

Guide:
"Every part of your story… I am there."

Scene 5: "Every Good Thing Points to Me"

(Verse 10.41)

(They see famous people helping others, a mother comforting a child, a soldier protecting his country.)

Aryan:
"All these people are great in different ways."

Guide:
"Yes. Wherever you see power, kindness, talent, wisdom, beauty—it's a spark of My glory."

Scene 6: "No End to My Wonders"

(Verse 10.42)

Maya (wide-eyed):
"So... You're in *everything awesome*?!"

Guide:
"Yes, but this is just a tiny part of My wonder. Keep your eyes open, and you'll always find Me."

Final Scene: "The Real Treasure"

(Back in their room. The map dissolves into golden light.)

Aryan:
"We didn't find gold or diamonds."

Maya:
"But we found the real treasure: Seeing God in everything!"

Grandma Gita (appearing magically):
"That, my dears, is the treasure the Gita shares."

Moral of the Story:

True devotion begins when we see God's presence in everything beautiful, wise, strong, or kind. The world is full of His sparks—if we have the eyes to see.

Allegory Table:

Verse	Bhagavad Gita Meaning	Modern Allegory/Metaphor

10.1–4	Krishna reveals divine wisdom	The glowing treasure map and Cosmic Guide
10.8–10	Source of everything, devotion with love	Seed growing, stars forming
10.11	Destroys ignorance with light of knowledge	Brain cave lighting up
10.19–39	I am the best among categories	Sun, thunderbolt, Garuda, fig tree, scientist
10.41	Wherever there is greatness, I am there	Heroes, helpers, talent in every field
10.42	My glories are infinite	The map dissolves, infinite wonder remains

Chapter 10

Title10a: "The Great Talent Show - Discovering the Divine Spark"

Characters:

- **Aarav (Arjuna)** – Curious, now full of questions about talents and abilities
- **Krish Sir (Krishna)** – Wise mentor and guide
- **Sneha** – Aarav's younger sister, artistic and innocent
- **Principal Vedaji** – The mysterious school principal (represents the Divine)
- **Various students** – Each with a unique talent or gift

- **Science Club, Art Club, Drama Club** – Representing various fields of excellence

Scene 1: The Question About Greatness (Verses 1–3)

Location: School Library

Aarav (curious): "Krish Sir, you say the Divine is in everything. But… how do I know where He shines the most?"

Krish Sir (smiling): "Ah! Now you're ready to know the **vibhutis**—the special sparks of the Divine."

Metaphor: The divine is like electricity—present in all, but glowing brighter in some places.

Scene 2: The Origin of All (Verses 4–6)

Krish Sir (to students in Science Club): "Who gave us intelligence, memory, patience, and courage? These are not just *skills*, they are *gifts* from the source of life."

Sneha (thoughtfully): "So... even kindness is a gift?"

Krish Sir: "Yes, and the one who gives these gifts is present in all beings, silently."

Allegory: Talents are rays of the same sun, expressed differently in each.

Scene 3: The Unseen Friend (Verses 7–11)

Aarav (while helping Sneha rehearse): "Sometimes I feel guided by something... like someone is whispering answers during tough times."

Krish Sir: "That's the inner guide. The more you love and remember, the more it reveals."

Sneha: "Is it like how the torch in the dark shows only what we need?"

Krish Sir: "Exactly! Divine guidance is like that torch."

Metaphor: The Divine lights the path for those who seek with love.

Scene 4: Glimpses of Divine Spark – Talent Show Begins! (Verses 12–20)

Location: The School's Great Annual Talent Show – "Divine Within"

Each student steps up with a unique performance:

- **Ravi** recites poetry (Divine through speech)
- **Asha** sings (Divine through music)
- **Kiran** shows amazing memory skills (Divine through knowledge)

- **Tara** does martial arts (Divine through strength)
- **Sneha** paints (Divine through creativity)

Krish Sir (watching all): “All these talents—poetry, art, wisdom—are expressions of the same unseen spark.”

Aarav: “So God is not just in temples… He’s also in talents?”

Krish Sir: “Yes. Wherever you see something extraordinary—it’s a *vibhuti*, a sparkle of the Divine.”

Allegory: God expresses through brilliance in nature, humans, and acts.

Scene 5: A World Full of Glories (Verses 21–39)

Krish Sir leads Aarav through the school garden at sunset.

Krish Sir: “Among stars, I’m the Sun. Among rivers, I’m the Ganga. Among warriors, I’m the bravest. Among letters, I’m the ‘A’. Among seasons, I’m spring.”

Aarav (awed): “Wow… You mean every great thing is like a clue pointing to the divine?”

Krish Sir: “Yes! These glories are not just things—they are *signposts* to the Source.”

Metaphor: Divine shines brightest in the best of each category.

Scene 6: All Comes from Me (Verses 40–42)

Krish Sir (closing ceremony): "But Aarav, remember—these are just glimpses. The full Divine can't be seen in parts. Everything you admire… comes from the Whole."

Aarav (smiling): "Then every talent, every good deed, every beautiful thing—is a piece of that greatness?"

Krish Sir (placing a hand on Aarav's shoulder): "Yes. And that greatness lives inside you too."

Allegory Table:

Verse Range	Allegory/Story Element	Metaphor
10.1–3	Krish Sir talks about unseen greatness	Secret spark of Divine in all things
10.4–6	Talents and virtues discussed in Science Club	Talents = gifts from the same source
10.7–11	Inner voice as guide	Divine = torchlight in dark moments
10.12–20	Talent show scenes	Every excellence =

		Divine expression
10.21–39	"Among rivers, I'm Ganga…" list shared	Divine shines brightest in best of all
10.40–42	Everything from One Whole	All beauty, power, and wisdom = from the same Source

Kids' Insights & Takeaways

1. **Everyone has a special spark** – Your talents are divine gifts.
2. **Admire and respect excellence** – It connects you to the Divine.
3. **The Divine is not far—it's within you** – in your thoughts, actions, and efforts.
4. **No one is small** – Every person has a unique glory.
5. **Appreciating beauty, power, and knowledge leads you to deeper understanding of life.**

Chapter 11

Title11: "Aryan and the Cosmic VR Headset"

Main Characters:

- **Aryan** – A curious 12-year-old boy who seeks the truth
- **Grandma Gita** – The wise grandmother (representing Krishna)
- **Maya** – Aryan's adventurous cousin
- **The Universal VR Guide** – A mystical narrator inside the VR headset

Theme

When we truly see the universe as it is—vast, mysterious, powerful, and full of divine energy—we are both amazed and humbled. The Divine exists in all forms—both peaceful and terrifying. The key is surrendering to that Supreme Truth with love and faith.

Scene 1: "The Wish to See Everything"

(Verse 11.1–4)

(Aryan and Maya are in their room with Grandma Gita. She hands them a futuristic-looking headset.)

Aryan:
"Grandma, you always say God is everywhere. I want to see how!"

Grandma Gita (smiling):
"Are you ready for the truth? Here—put this on. But be warned—what you see may change how you see the world forever."

Scene 2: "Divine Eyes Activated"

(Verse 11.5–8)

(Aryan puts on the headset. Everything goes black. A voice booms: "Welcome to the Vishwarupa Experience. Divine Vision Activated.")

VR Guide:
"You will now see the infinite. But mortal eyes alone cannot handle it. I give you divine sight!"

(Aryan's eyes glow. He sees galaxies spinning, time folding, and endless stars.)

Scene 3: "The Cosmic Form Revealed"

(Verse 11.9–15)

(Suddenly, Aryan sees a gigantic being—made of stars, oceans, animals, time, fire, and space—all woven together.)

Aryan (gasping):
"Is this... God? It's everything at once!"

Maya (watching from outside the headset):
"What do you see?!"

Aryan:
"A thousand suns rising… lions roaring… planets dancing. It's beautiful… but also scary!"

Scene 4: "The Terrifying Truth"

(Verse 11.23–30)

(The form now begins to consume galaxies, warriors, and even time itself in its fiery mouth.)

Aryan (trembling):
"Why is it… destroying everything?"

VR Guide:
"I am Time. I come to destroy so that creation can continue. All beings must pass through Me."

(Aryan sees familiar faces—selfish leaders, proud heroes—all being absorbed by the flames.)

Scene 5: "Overwhelmed and Awed"

(Verse 11.31–35)

Aryan (falling to his knees):
"I can't handle this! You are beyond everything I imagined! What should I do?"

VR Guide:
"Stand up. Do your duty. I have already planned the outcome. You are just My instrument."

Scene 6: "The Request for Forgiveness"

(Verse 11.36–45)

(Aryan thinks of the times he joked, argued, or ignored God's presence.)

Aryan (hands folded):
"O Great One! Please forgive me. I didn't know who You truly were. I spoke to You like a friend… not realizing You are all that exists!"

Scene 7: "The Return to Gentle Form"

(Verse 11.46–50)

(The terrifying form dissolves, and a gentle, kind figure of light appears.)

VR Guide (smiling):
"I show both faces—the fierce and the friendly. Now you have seen My truth. Fear not."

Final Scene: "Surrender and Peace"

(Verse 11.55)

Aryan (removing the headset):
"I thought God was just a kind friend. But now I know—He's everything. He gives, He takes, and He loves."

Grandma Gita:
"When you understand this, and serve with no ego or selfishness, He protects you forever."

Moral of the Story:

God is not just a cute statue or a friendly cloud. He is the whole universe—terrifying and loving, powerful and peaceful. True devotion means doing your duty with love and surrendering to the Divine's plan.

Allegory Table:

Verse	Gita Essence	Story Element / Metaphor
11.1–4	Arjuna asks to see God's universal form	Aryan asks Grandma for a divine vision
11.5–8	Krishna gives divine vision	VR headset gives 'Divine Eyes'

11.9–15	Arjuna sees the universal form	Cosmic Form of galaxies, animals, time
11.23–30	Form becomes terrifying and destructive	Beings being consumed by fire and time
11.31–35	Arjuna fears and asks what to do	Aryan realizes he's just an instrument
11.36–45	Arjuna asks forgiveness	Aryan reflects on how he treated the Divine lightly
11.46–50	Krishna returns to gentle form	VR Form becomes calm, reassuring light
11.55	Final verse: Bhakti brings peace	Grandma says surrender and love are key

Chapter 11

Title11a: "The Cosmic Spectacle - Seeing Beyond What Eyes Can See"

Main Characters:

- **Aarav (Arjuna)** – Still on his learning journey; full of questions
- **Krish Sir (Krishna)** – The wise, loving guide revealing deeper truths
- **Sneha** – Aarav's younger sister, innocent and artistic
- **Principal Vedaji** – A symbolic figure of the Universal Divine
- **Students and Teachers** – Witnesses of the event

Scene 1: "I Want to See!" (Verses 1–4)

Location: School Auditorium, before a big science-art-tech exhibition.

Aarav (with curiosity): "Krish Sir, you told me about the divine spark in everything... but I want to *see* it. Not just believe it."

Krish Sir (nodding): "Aarav, you're ready. But know this — what you will see is not ordinary. It's the **Vishwarupa**, the Universal Form."

Allegory: Aarav represents the seeker ready to see the *whole truth*.

Scene 2: "You Need Special Vision" (Verses 5–8)

Krish Sir gives Aarav **a virtual reality headset**—not just any headset, but one that "shows the truth behind appearances."

Krish Sir (softly): "With your eyes, you see limits. With this, you'll see the limitless."

Sneha (wide-eyed): "Is it like magic?"

Krish Sir: "More than magic — it's *reality* in full."

Metaphor: The headset = divine wisdom that helps us perceive the whole.

Scene 3: "The Cosmic Form Appears!" (Verses 9–14)

Aarav puts on the headset.

Suddenly the auditorium disappears. Aarav is standing in a **cosmic space** — stars spinning, galaxies flowing, time ticking, life birthing and ending — all inside **one massive, radiant figure**.

He sees rivers flowing from hands, fire in eyes, sun and moon as eyes, and thousands of forms in one.

Aarav (trembling): "What… is this…?"

Allegory: The Universe itself as the body of the Divine.

Scene 4: "Time, Power, and Awe" (Verses 15–31)

Aarav watches as time flows through the cosmic form — **creatures being born, growing, aging, and dissolving**.

He sees kings, scientists, artists, even himself—part of a massive play, each person like a spark.

Suddenly, he sees forms being **devoured by fire** from the divine's mouth — not out of cruelty, but to show the **truth of impermanence**.

Aarav (crying): "Is this… God?"

Krish Sir's voice echoes in the cosmic world: "Yes, I am Time. I destroy so that creation continues. I am not just sweet — I am the truth."

Metaphor: Time and transformation are also divine acts.

Scene 5: "Aarav's Realization" (Verses 32–44)

Aarav (falling to his knees in the vision): "I mocked… I doubted… I called you 'Sir', joked with you, never realizing who you were. Forgive me."

Krish Sir appears in the cosmic form, smiling gently.

Krish Sir: "Aarav, love makes Me playful. Wisdom makes Me powerful. Both are Me."

Allegory: The seeker surrenders, recognizing the divine in all roles — teacher, friend, destroyer, protector.

Scene 6: "Back to Normal" (Verses 45–55)

The headset is removed.

Aarav is back in the auditorium. But he sees **everything differently** now.

He looks at **Sneha painting**, a **janitor sweeping**, a **bird outside** — and whispers:

Aarav: “You’re all… part of Him.”

Krish Sir (smiling): “Now you know. Don’t fear greatness. Don’t fear change. Serve with love, and remember: the Divine is everywhere, and also within you.”

Allegory & Metaphor Table – Chapter 11

Verse Range	Allegory/Story Element	Metaphor
11.1–4	Aarav asks to see the Divine	Seeker asking for deeper truth
11.5–8	Krish Sir gives VR headset	Divine wisdom needed to perceive truth
11.9–14	Cosmic form revealed	Universe = Body of the Divine
11.15–31	Creation/destruction in divine form	Time = divine force; everything flows through Him
11.32–44	Aarav surrenders	Realization of Divine’s vastness and roles

11.45–55	Return to normal vision, deeper awareness	Seeing God in the everyday

Kids' Insights & Takeaways

1. **There's more than meets the eye** – Truth goes beyond what you see.
2. **The Universe is divine** – The Creator and Creation are one.
3. **Respect all roles of life** – God is not only kind and sweet but also the transformer.
4. **Be humble** – Even a friend or teacher can carry a higher purpose.
5. **True devotion comes with awe and understanding** – Not just blind belief.

Chapter 12

Title12: "Tanu and the Treasure of the Heart"

Characters:

- **Tanu** – A thoughtful and kind 12-year-old girl
- **Grandpa Dev** – Her wise grandfather (symbol of Lord Krishna)
- **Ravi** – Her older brother, very logical and brainy
- **Mystic Voice** – A guiding inner voice during Tanu's dream
- **The Heart Mirror** – A magical device in her dream

Theme (Chapter 12 Summary for Kids):

Devotion is more powerful than knowledge alone. God loves those who serve with a pure heart, without pride or hate, with calmness and kindness. It's not how clever we are, but how lovingly we live.

Scene 1: "Brains or Heart?"

(Verses 12.1–2)

(Tanu and Ravi are walking in the garden with Grandpa Dev.)

Ravi (grinning):
"Grandpa, is it better to study God through science and facts or through prayer and love?"

Tanu (smiling):
"I think it's better to love God like a friend."

Grandpa Dev:
"Ah, what a question! Some worship the invisible Truth, some worship Me directly with love. Both paths reach the same place… but the path of love is easier and dearer."

Scene 2: "The Dream Challenge"

(Verses 12.3–7)

(That night, Tanu has a dream. She enters a strange world and hears a Mystic Voice.)

Mystic Voice:
"You must reach the treasure of peace. You

may choose the Path of the Mind or the Path of the Heart."

(Ravi appears on a floating boat with books and gadgets — "Mind Path.")

(Tanu chooses the bridge of glowing hearts — "Heart Path.")

Scene 3: "Obstacles and Help"

(Verses 12.8–12)

(Tanu walks calmly, singing a song of love, helping creatures along the way — a lost bunny, a crying robot, and a frozen flower.)

Mystic Voice (softly):
"You may not know the scriptures, but your love, care, and service are enough. Do what you can, with devotion."

Scene 4: "The Mirror Test"

(Verses 12.13–19)

(Tanu reaches a magical mirror — "The Heart Mirror" — that shows her true nature.)

Mirror Voice:
"Only those with a pure heart can pass. Let's see..."

- *She sees herself forgiving her friend who lied (Verse 12.13 – "free from hate").*

- *She sees herself helping Ravi even when he teased her (Verse 12.14 – "forgiving and friendly").*
- *She sees herself being calm during her math test panic (Verse 12.15 – "not disturbed").*

Mirror Voice:
"You are dear to the Divine. Enter the Garden of Peace."

Scene 5: "The Garden of Peace"

(Verse 12.20)

(Tanu enters a bright garden full of colors, music, and calm breeze. A glowing figure greets her—it's Grandpa Dev in divine form.)

Divine Grandpa:
"Those who live with love, no pride, no anger, and steady faith are My favorites. You are one of them."

Scene 6: "Back to the Real World"

(Morning – Tanu wakes up with a smile.)

Tanu (to Ravi):
"Being smart is cool, but being loving and calm is even better!"

Grandpa Dev (winking):

"And now you've truly understood Bhakti Yoga — the yoga of the heart."

Allegory Table

Verse(s)	Gita Wisdom	Story Symbol
12.1–2	Two paths: worship with form or formless	Tanu's choice between Heart Path and Mind Path
12.3–7	Devotion with love is easiest	Tanu walks the heart path and serves others
12.8–12	Start with full devotion, or just do your duty	Tanu sings, serves, and loves in small ways
12.13–19	Who is dear to God? The one who is humble, kind	Mirror reveals her acts of patience, kindness
12.20	Devotees of Bhakti Yoga are dearest to God	Tanu enters the peaceful garden of divine love

Moral of the Story:

God does not ask us to be perfect. He asks us to love, forgive, stay calm, help others, and believe with our heart. Even small actions done with love are powerful.

Chapter 12

Title12a: "The Heart That Connects"

Main Characters:

- **Aarav** – Now more awakened, seeking deeper understanding
- **Krish Sir** – The wise teacher, now more visibly divine
- **Sneha** – Aarav's younger sister, pure-hearted and devoted
- **Principal Vedaji** – Symbol of the Divine Presence in all
- **Classmates** – Represent different paths and attitudes toward truth

Scene 1: "What's the Best Way?" (Verses 1–5)

Location: School garden, under the banyan tree.

Aarav (serious): "Krish Sir, some meditate on the invisible, others love God like a friend. Which is better?"

Krish Sir (smiling): "Both paths lead to Me, Aarav. But the path of love, devotion, and surrender – **bhakti** – is the easiest for hearts like yours."

Sneha (sitting nearby, humming a devotional tune): "So I can love God like I love Mom?"

Krish Sir (gently): "Yes, dear Sneha. Just like that. Simple and pure."

Metaphor: Bhakti is like a child's love – effortless and trusting.

Scene 2: "Understanding Bhakti" (Verses 6–12)

Classmate 1 (curious): "So if I don't know how to meditate, I can still connect with God?"

Krish Sir: "Yes. If you can't meditate, serve. If you can't serve, offer your work. If you can't do that, just surrender with faith. *Even a small offering with devotion reaches Me.*"

Aarav (in awe): "You mean… even drawing with love is devotion?"

Krish Sir: "Exactly. The feeling matters more than the form."

Allegory: A small flower offered with love is greater than gold offered with pride.

Scene 3: "What Makes Someone Dear to God?" (Verses 13–20)

Krish Sir walks among the students, his presence calm and glowing.

Krish Sir: "Let Me tell you who is dearest to Me…"

Soft music plays as He recites qualities:

- **One who is kind and does not hate**
- **One who is content and steady**
- **One who forgives and is free from selfishness**
- **One who is not shaken by ups and downs**
- **One who is humble, silent, and full of love**

Sneha (eyes wide): "Krish Sir, I want to be that person!"

Aarav: "But it's so hard to be perfect…"

Krish Sir (gently): "You don't need to be perfect. Just try… and love."

Metaphor: Devotion is like watering a plant daily – small efforts grow into something beautiful.

Scene 4: "Aarav's Silent Devotion" (Closing Scene)

Later that evening, Aarav sits by the window with a diary.

He writes:

"Dear Krish Sir,
Today I didn't meditate, or study deeply.
But I helped Sneha with her drawing,
I listened to a friend who was sad,
I forgave someone who hurt me.
Is that also devotion?"

Wind blows gently. A page flips. Krish Sir's voice echoes in his heart:

"Yes, Aarav. That *is* devotion.
When love fills your actions, I am already with you."

Allegory Table:

Verse Range	Allegory/Story Element	Metaphor
12.1–5	Choosing between paths	Devotion is like a child's love – natural & pure

12.6–12	Gradual steps to devotion	Watering a plant – effort matters
12.13–20	Qualities of a true devotee	Heart over ritual – gentle, humble, kind

Kids' Insights & Takeaways

1. **Devotion isn't only about rituals** – It's in kindness, forgiveness, and love.
2. **Even small acts matter** – Helping, sharing, forgiving are all forms of bhakti.
3. **You don't need to be perfect** – Just try, and let your heart lead.
4. **God sees your effort, not your success** – Intention is greater than outcome.
5. **Bhakti is for everyone** – It doesn't need age, money, or rituals—just a loving heart.

Chapter 13

Title13: "Riya and the Secret Garden"

A journey of discovering the body, mind, and the soul through a magical adventure.

Characters:

- **Riya** – A curious and thoughtful 12-year-old girl
- **Grandma Anandi** – Wise and loving, represents divine wisdom (Krishna)
- **The Garden Spirit** – Mysterious voice and guide inside the dream world
- **Mirror Tree** – Magical tree that reflects truth
- **The Field Creatures** – Emotions like Anger, Joy, Sadness (represent qualities of the Kshetra)
- **The Observer** – Glowing silent figure watching the garden (symbol of the Knower/Soul)

Core Idea:

The body and mind are like a field where different emotions and actions grow (Kshetra). But you are not the field—you are the one who watches, learns, and grows beyond it (Kshetrajna).

Scene 1: "The Puzzle of the Field"

(Verse 13.1–2)

(Riya sits with Grandma Anandi in the backyard garden.)

Riya:
"Grandma, sometimes I feel angry, scared, or even super happy. But other times, I feel like I'm just... watching all of it. Who am I really?"

Grandma (smiling):
"You are not the garden, my dear. You are the one who sees it. The body is like a field. You are the one who knows the field."

Riya:
"Wait… like a gardener?"

Grandma:
"Exactly. Let's see where your dream takes you tonight."

Scene 2: "The Dream Garden"

(Verses 13.3–6)

(Riya falls asleep and finds herself in a magical garden called 'The Field.' Trees whisper, rivers sing, and colors swirl.)

Garden Spirit (voice):
"This is your Kshetra — your body, mind, thoughts, and feelings. Look closely. Everything grows here."

(She sees Joy jumping around, Anger throwing stones, Curiosity asking questions, and Fear hiding.)

Riya:
"Wow! These are my feelings?"

Garden Spirit:
"Yes. But don't forget… You are not them. You are the one seeing them."

Scene 3: "The Mirror Tree"

(Verses 13.7–11 – Qualities for spiritual understanding)

(Riya approaches a shimmering tree with hanging mirrors. Each mirror shows a different version of her.)

- *One shows her yelling at her brother.*
- *One shows her helping a lost puppy.*
- *One shows her afraid in class.*

Mirror Tree:
"To truly know the garden, you must practice humility, forgiveness, peace, and faith."

Riya (thinking):
"If I keep watching my feelings and stay calm, maybe I can take care of the garden better."

Scene 4: "The Silent Observer"

(Verse 13.12–17 – The Soul or Divine presence)

(A glowing figure appears above the garden, still and peaceful. It watches the chaos and joy silently.)

Riya (whispering):
"Who is that?"

Garden Spirit:
"That is the Knower. The Divine within all. It sees everything, touches nothing. It is inside your heart, and in every garden."

Riya:
"So I'm not just my body or feelings. I'm also... that peaceful watcher?"

Garden Spirit:
"Yes. And so is everyone else."

Scene 5: "Everyone Has a Garden"

(Verses 13.18–23 – Soul in all beings)

(Riya walks through different gardens – Ravi's, her teacher's, even the school bully's – all with similar Field Creatures but different moods.)

Riya (softly):
"Everyone has their own garden. Some are messy, some are calm. But we all have the same Silent Observer inside."

Scene 6: "The Awakening"

(Verse 13.24–35 – Realizing the eternal soul)

(The garden begins to glow. Riya feels light and peaceful. She hears Grandma's voice calling from afar.)

Garden Spirit:
"Remember, take care of your garden, but never forget—you are more than it. You are the gardener and the watcher."

(Riya wakes up smiling, eyes wide open.)

Riya (to Grandma):
"I'm going to be a peaceful gardener from now on!"

Allegory Table:

Verse(s)	Bhagavad Gita Teaching	Story Symbol

13.1–2	Kshetra (field) and Kshetrajna (knower of field)	Garden and Riya as the gardener
13.3–6	Body and mind are the field	Garden with emotional creatures
13.7–11	Qualities for self-realization	Mirror Tree with virtues
13.12–17	Divine Soul beyond the visible	The glowing Observer watching silently
13.18–23	Soul in all beings	Riya visits other gardens (other people's minds)
13.24–35	Liberation through understanding	Realization and waking up with awareness

Moral of the Story:

You are not your thoughts, feelings, or even your body. You are the loving gardener of your inner world—and a peaceful soul watching over it all. Be kind to your own garden, and to everyone else's too.

Chapter 13

Title13a: "The Map and the Explorer"

Theme:

This chapter explains the difference between **"Kṣetra" (the Field = body & mind)** and **"Kṣetrajña" (the Knower = the true Self)** using metaphors and stories. Perfect for a thoughtful, magical tale!

Characters:

- **Aarav** – Curious seeker, now more mature
- **Sneha** – Innocent little sister, full of questions
- **Krish Sir** – Wise teacher (representation of Krishna)
- **Robo-Buddy** – A school-made robot for the science fair (represents the body/field)
- **The Inner Voice** – Representation of the soul/consciousness

Scene 1: “The Robot Science Fair” (Verses 1–3)

Setting: School auditorium, buzzing with excitement.

Sneha: "Aarav, your robot looks real! Does it *think*?"

Aarav (laughs): "It does everything I program it to. But it doesn’t *know* itself."

Krish Sir walks in smiling.

Krish Sir: "Exactly, Aarav. The robot is the ‘**field**’ – it can act, move, sense. But YOU are the ‘**knower**’ – the one who *experiences* and *understands*.”

Metaphor: The robot is like our body & mind – the *field*. But the one observing it – that’s YOU, the soul.

Scene 2: “Mapping the Field” (Verses 4–7)

Krish Sir points to a big digital screen showing brain, nerves, heart, emotions, memory.

Krish Sir: “This entire system – thoughts, pain, joy, actions, desires – is the field. It's like a **map**.”

Sneha (confused): "So I'm just the map?"

Krish Sir (grins): "No, Sneha. You are the **explorer** using the map. The map shows the world, but YOU walk the path."

Allegory: The body is a map; the soul is the traveler.

Scene 3: "Seeing with Inner Eyes" (Verses 8–11)

Classmate (overhearing): "How can we know the difference between the map and the explorer?"

Krish Sir: "Through **humility, patience, forgiveness, and focus**, you start seeing clearly. That's called **Jnana** – real knowledge."

Sneha (closes her eyes): "I feel something when I'm kind or quiet inside. Is that... the knower?"

Krish Sir: "Yes, Sneha. That is your **true self** – shining silently."

Metaphor: Knowledge is like a flashlight in the dark—showing what's real.

Scene 4: "The Soul in All" (Verses 12–17)

Krish Sir points to everyone in the hall.

Krish Sir: "Though every robot looks different, they all need the same **power source**. Just like that, every person has the **same soul spark** within."

Aarav (eyes widening): "So... we're all different *outside*, but the same *inside*?"

Krish Sir: "Exactly. The soul is **in all**, beyond caste, name, or talent."

Metaphor: Just like electricity powers every device, the same divine spark powers every life.

Scene 5: "The Invisible Knower" (Verses 18–23)

Robo-Buddy suddenly shuts down.

Sneha (sad): "It's not moving!"

Krish Sir: "The *knower* behind it – Aarav's code and energy – is no longer operating it. Like that, when the soul leaves, the body doesn't work."

Aarav (reflects): "We are not the machine… We are the one inside, watching and guiding."

Scene 6: "Becoming Wise Explorers" (Verses 24–35)

Krish Sir gathers the children for one last message.

Krish Sir: "Some realize the truth through meditation. Some through learning. Some just by serving others."

Sneha: "What if I just love everyone and help when I can?"

Krish Sir (smiling): "Then you're already walking the path of light."

Allegory Table:

Verse Range	Allegory / Story Element	Metaphor
13.1–3	Robot and Programmer	Field = Body; Knower = Programmer/Soul
13.4–7	Map and Explorer	Body = Map; Soul = Explorer
13.8–11	Values of the Seeker	Knowledge = Flashlight showing truth
13.12–17	Soul in All	Electricity in all bulbs = Soul in all bodies

13.18–23	Robot shutdown	Soul's presence = Energy making the body work
13.24–35	Different paths to truth	All rivers flow into one ocean

Kids' Takeaways and Reflections

1. **You are not your body or thoughts** – You are the observer inside.
2. **Everyone has the same light** – Be kind and respectful to all.
3. **Even a robot can't work without a programmer** – Your body needs your soul.
4. **Knowing yourself brings peace** – Be mindful, calm, and loving.
5. **You can find truth in your own way** – Through love, learning, or service.

Chapter 14

Title14: "The Three Paintbrushes"

An artistic journey through the world of qualities—Sattva, Rajas, and Tamas.

Characters:

- **Meera** – A creative, curious 12-year-old girl who loves to paint
- **Grandpa Veer** – A wise old artist (symbolizing Krishna)
- **Three Paintbrushes** – Magical talking brushes named Sattva (golden), Rajas (red), and Tamas (black)
- **Painting World** – A dreamland where Meera enters to paint her inner self
- **The Voice of Truth** – A silent shining figure in the sky (symbol of the Supreme Self)

Core Idea:

All living beings are influenced by **three qualities**:

- **Sattva (Goodness/Light)** – calm, wise, happy
- **Rajas (Passion/Movement)** – active, restless, ambitious
- **Tamas (Darkness/Inertia)** – sleepy, lazy, confused
  The one who sees all three but is beyond them becomes truly free.

Scene 1: "The Artist's Challenge"

(Verse 14.1–3)

(Meera sits in Grandpa Veer's art room.)

Meera:
"Grandpa, you always say that painting teaches us about life. But how?"

Grandpa Veer:
"There are three magical paintbrushes hidden in my studio. Each one shows you a different world inside you. Do you want to try?"

Meera (excited):
"Yes! Let's begin!"

Scene 2: "The World of Paint"

(Verse 14.4–5)

(As Meera touches an old canvas, she is sucked into a colorful world. Three brushes float before her.)

Golden Brush (Sattva):
"I bring peace, wisdom, and light."

Red Brush (Rajas):
"I bring energy, desire, and action!"

Black Brush (Tamas):
"I bring rest, silence... or confusion."

(A glowing sun appears above.)
Voice:
"These are the *gunas*, the qualities in all beings. They arise from nature, but you are more than them."

Scene 3: "Sattva – The Peaceful Meadow"

(Verses 14.6–8)

(Meera uses the golden brush and enters a peaceful meadow. Butterflies dance, animals rest calmly.)

Sattva Brush:
"In this world, minds are clear, hearts are kind, and learning flows like a stream."

Meera:
"I feel so happy and focused here!"

Sattva Brush (gently):
"But beware—even peace can make you proud of being good."

Scene 4: "Rajas – The City of Racing Dreams"

(Verses 14.9–12)

(With the red brush, Meera steps into a buzzing city—traffic, ambition, shouting, goals everywhere.)

Rajas Brush:
"Here, everyone is chasing something—fame, success, likes, scores!"

Meera (overwhelmed):
"I feel excited, but also... tired."

Rajas Brush:
"That's what I do—desire drives action, but never rests."

Scene 5: "Tamas – The Foggy Forest"

(Verses 14.8–10)

(She now paints with the black brush—everything turns dark, sleepy, foggy. She hears whispers of doubt.)

Tamas Brush:
"Sleep, forget, hide from pain. Who needs effort anyway?"

Meera (struggling):
"I can't think clearly here. Everything is so slow."

Scene 6: "The Battle of the Brushes"

(Verse 14.11–13)

(All three brushes start fighting for her attention. The world keeps changing—peaceful, busy, sleepy—over and over again.)

Meera:
"Stop! I don't know which one to choose!"

Voice of Truth (from above):
"They all influence you. But you are not them. You are the painter who chooses."

Scene 7: "Beyond the Brushes"

(Verses 14.19–20)

(Meera drops all the brushes and sits quietly. She sees a glowing light rising within her heart.)

Voice of Truth:
"When you observe the qualities without becoming them, you become free. Be like the sky—watch the weather, but don't become the storm."

Meera (calmly):
"I'm not just what I feel or do... I am the one who watches."

Scene 8: "Returning to the Studio"

(Verses 14.23–27)

(Meera wakes up in Grandpa's studio, holding a new brush of clear light.)

Grandpa Veer:
"You've seen the three brushes. What did you learn?"

Meera:
"I'm not just my moods or actions. I'm the one who paints. And now I'll paint with peace, passion, and rest—but not let them control me."

Allegory Table – Chapter 14 Summary

Verse(s)	Bhagavad Gita Teaching	Story Element
14.1–3	The divine origin of the three gunas	Grandpa and entry into Paint World
14.4–5	All beings are born from nature	Magical brushes from the canvas
14.6–8	Nature of Sattva, Rajas, and Tamas	Three different worlds painted by brushes
14.9–13	How gunas bind and dominate	Brushes fighting for control
14.14–18	Destiny shaped by the dominant guna	Worlds shifting based on brushes used
14.19–20	Seeing beyond the gunas	Meera observing quietly
14.21–27	Path to transcendence	Clear light brush and wise realization

Moral of the Story:

Your moods, actions, and feelings are like paint colors. But you are the painter. Choose wisely, observe mindfully, and paint your life with awareness and balance.

Chapter 14

Title14a: "The Magic Paints: Sattva, Rajas & Tamas"

Theme:

This chapter explains how **three invisible qualities** (called **Gunas**)—**Sattva** (Purity), **Rajas** (Activity), and **Tamas** (Inertia)—influence how we think, act, and live. These are like **colors** that tint everything in our world.

Characters:

- **Aarav** – Curious student, now more thoughtful
- **Sneha** – Little sister, full of wonder
- **Krish Sir** – Wise teacher (Krishna's role)
- **Riya** – Classmate, loves art
- **The Gunas** – Appearing as magical **color fairies**

- **Sattva** – Dressed in white, glowing light
- **Rajas** – Dressed in red, fast and fiery
- **Tamas** – Dressed in dark blue, sleepy and still

Scene 1: “The Art Competition” (Verses 1–3)

Setting: School announces a magical art competition where colors choose the artist.

Krish Sir: “This art contest is special. The paints will guide your brush!”

Aarav: “Wait... What? The paints guide *me*?”

Krish Sir: “Yes. Just like life—three invisible energies guide your thoughts and actions. Let me introduce them…”

Metaphor: The world is like a canvas, and your mind is painted by three invisible colors—Sattva, Rajas, and Tamas.

Scene 2: “Meeting the Color Fairies” (Verses 4–9)

The stage transforms magically. The three fairies appear.

- **Sattva Fairy:** “I bring clarity, wisdom, and peace.”

- **Rajas Fairy:** “I bring desire, action, ambition. But beware—I'm never still.”
- **Tamas Fairy:** “I bring rest, sleep, laziness… but I also confuse and delay.”

Riya: “So... which one is the best?”

Krish Sir: “They all exist in everyone. One may dominate, but all are there.”

Allegory: These fairies are the Gunas. They are like inner artists who paint your personality every moment.

Scene 3: “Painting the World” (Verses 10–13)

Three kids start painting. Their styles differ.

- **Riya (with Sattva):** “My painting shows the sunrise, kindness, and learning.” *(She looks calm and joyful.)*
- **Sneha (with Rajas):** “Mine has fireworks, racing cars, and trophies!” *(She's excited but restless.)*
- **Another student (with Tamas):** “I painted… a dark cave. And… I'm sleepy.”

Krish Sir: “Each painting reflects their inner state. Your Guna chooses your lens.”

Metaphor: Like glasses with different tints—your Guna decides how you *see* the world.

Scene 4: "Where Do Gunas Take Us?" (Verses 14–18)

Krish Sir shows three staircases.

- **Sattva Stairs:** Lead upward to light, learning, and peace.
- **Rajas Stairs:** Go sideways—fast but noisy, leading to desire and stress.
- **Tamas Stairs:** Spiral downward into confusion, anger, and laziness.

Aarav: "What if I want to climb the light stairs?"

Krish Sir: "Then strengthen your Sattva—by learning, helping, meditating, being calm."

Allegory: Each Guna leads to a different outcome. Choose wisely.

Scene 5: "Beyond the Colors" (Verses 19–27)

Sattva Fairy steps forward.

Sattva: "Even I am a color. To reach your true self, you must go **beyond all three**."

Aarav (surprised): "Even you? Then what lies beyond?"

Krish Sir (gently): "Beyond the Gunas lies **freedom**. The soul, untouched and pure."

Sneha: "How do we go beyond?"

Krish Sir: “By seeing everything equally, not reacting, serving without expecting. You become peaceful inside.”

Metaphor: When you see all colors clearly, you realize the canvas is **always white beneath**.

Final Scene: “The True Artist”

All kids are called to present their paintings.

Aarav (shows blank canvas): “I wiped mine clean. Because I realized—I am not just the painter... I’m the one **watching** the painting.”

Krish Sir (smiling): “Brilliant. You’ve seen through the illusion.”

"In the temple of creation, while all the painters rush to fill their canvases with color and emotion, one soul sits quietly, observing. Their canvas is blank — not out of lack, but out of fullness. It holds the infinite within it, untouched, eternal. That is the Sattvic way — calm, content, witnessing the world without being entangled in it."

"I am not painting, I am just watching others paint" means:

- I am in a state of calm observation.
- I am detached from the need to act or create just for the sake of it.

- I am at peace, content in witnessing beauty without needing to possess it.

Allegory Table:

Verse Range	Allegory / Story Element	Metaphor
14.1–3	Magic art contest & invisible paint	Gunas influence every human action and feeling
14.4–9	Three fairies: Sattva, Rajas, Tamas	Purity, passion, and laziness within us
14.10–13	Different painting styles	Gunas shape perception and behavior
14.14–18	Three staircases	Each Guna leads to different destinations
14.19–27	Going beyond the Gunas	True freedom is knowing the soul, not being ruled by Gunas

Kids' Insights & Takeaways

1. **You are more than your moods and habits.**
   Gunas are like clothes you wear—not who you are.

2. **Sattva is the path of light.**
   Be calm, curious, kind, and giving.
3. **Rajas can make you restless.**
   Use your energy wisely. Don't chase only results.
4. **Tamas is sneaky.**
   Laziness, anger, or confusion can pull you down.
5. **You can go beyond all three.**
   Be peaceful, wise, and see all beings equally.

SATTVIC
RAJASIC
TAMASIC

Chapter 15

Title15: "The Tree of Twisted Reflections"

A journey through a mysterious world to discover the real self

Main Characters:

- **Anaya** – A smart and imaginative 12-year-old girl
- **Grandma Vaidehi** – A calm storyteller who guides Anaya (symbolizing Krishna)
- **Mirror Tree** – A magical upside-down tree with shiny leaves
- **Shadow Beings** – People lost in illusions, chasing reflections
- **The True Light** – A golden orb that shows the eternal soul

Allegory Table:

Concept	Metaphor Used
Samsara – Material existence	Inverted tree rooted in the sky
World entanglement	Reflection of the tree
Real Self (Atman)	Light beyond the reflection
Detachment & wisdom	Cutting the tree with knowledge
Supreme Self (Purushottama)	Light that sustains all beings

Scene 1: The Mirror Forest

(Verses 15.1–2)

Anaya (holding Grandma's hand):
"Grandma, why do I feel like life is so confusing? Sometimes I don't know what's real."

Grandma Vaidehi (smiling):
"To understand life, you must visit the Mirror Forest. Are you ready for an adventure?"

(They step into a glowing portal and enter a strange forest where a tree grows upside-down. Its roots are in the sky and branches below reflect in water.)

Anaya (amazed):
"Whoa! The tree is upside-down! Why?"

Grandma:
"This is the Tree of Life. The root is the Divine above. The branches below are all that we see—our dreams, our actions, our desires."

Scene 2: The People of Reflection

(Verses 15.3–5)

(Anaya sees people chasing shiny fruits on the branches, but they fall through illusions.)

Shadow Being:
"I just need more fruits—more praise, more toys, more followers!"

Anaya:
"But those are just reflections! The real fruits are above!"

Grandma:
"Yes, but they forget. That's how the soul gets stuck in this upside-down world."

Anaya:
"So how do we escape?"

Grandma (pulling out a golden axe):
"With the axe of knowledge. When you understand what's real and what's not, you cut the ties of illusion."

Scene 3: Remembering the Root

(Verse 15.6–7)

(Anaya looks up at the root glowing in the sky—a bright light.)

Anaya:
"That light… I feel like it's calling me."

Grandma:
"That's the source of everything. The real home. The soul (Atman) is a spark from that light."

(She sees herself glowing faintly inside.)

Anaya:
"So I'm not just this body? I'm part of that light?"

Grandma (nodding):
"And when you forget that, you get caught in the branches of desire, fear, and pride."

Scene 4: The Wandering Soul

(Verse 15.8–11)

(A soul-shaped bubble floats between bodies—an old man, a child, a dancer, a scholar.)

Grandma:
"The soul moves from body to body, just like wind carries fragrance from flower to flower."

Anaya:
"But why do some people understand and others don't?"

Grandma:
"Those who see with wisdom know the soul is separate from the body. The rest remain lost in reflections."

Scene 5: The Light Behind All

(Verse 15.12–15)

(Suddenly, day turns into night. The moon and sun glow brightly.)

Grandma (pointing to sun and moon):
"Even these shine with the power of the Supreme. Every breath, every thought, comes from that One."

Anaya:
"So the same light is in me, in the sun, and in others?"

Grandma:
"Yes. That light nourishes all. Remember it always."

Scene 6: The Eternal and the Temporary

(Verse 15.16–18)

(Two forms appear—one constantly changing, one still and shining.)

Grandma:
"There are two things in this world—what changes and what never does. The body changes. But your true self does not."

Anaya:
"And above both is… the Supreme Self?"

Grandma (smiling):
"Yes. That One is beyond change. Knowing that makes you wise."

Scene 7: The Return

(Verse 15.19–20)

(Anaya bows to the root of the tree. The forest starts to glow golden. The mirror tree fades.)

Anaya:
"I get it now! I'm not the reflection. I'm the light."

Grandma:
"And now you know the deepest secret. Always stay connected to the root above, not just the branches below."

(They walk out of the forest, hand in hand.)

Allegory Table:

Verse(s)	Gita Concept	Story Scene
15.1–2	Upside-down tree of life	Mirror Tree in the forest

15.3–5	Cutting the tree with knowledge	Golden axe of wisdom
15.6–7	Soul as a spark of divine light	Anaya sees the inner glow
15.8–11	Soul moves from body to body	Bubble soul floats through forms
15.12–15	God as the light in sun, moon, digestion	Nature glowing with divine energy
15.16–18	Perishable, imperishable, and Supreme	Two forms appear—change and eternity
15.19–20	One who knows the Supreme is wise	Anaya bows to the root, truth revealed

Moral of the Story:

Don't get lost in the reflections of life. Know your true light, stay connected to the root, and let wisdom guide you beyond illusions.

Chapter 15

Title15a: "The Inverted Tree and the Mirror of Truth"

Theme:

This chapter talks about the **Tree of Life**, which grows **upside down**, representing the material world. To reach **the Supreme Truth**, one must **cut through the illusion** and realize the eternal soul (Puruṣottama) that is beyond change.

Characters:

- **Aarav** – The curious boy, now more awakened
- **Sneha** – Little sister, cheerful and deep
- **Krish Sir** – Wise teacher (Krishna's role)
- **Tree Guardian** – Mysterious spirit who reveals the truth

- **Mirror Fairy** – Offers a mirror to reflect the true self
- **Other classmates** – Represent worldly attachments

Scene 1: "The Field Trip Begins" (Verses 1–2)

Setting: The class visits a mystical forest for their final school project.

Krish Sir: "Today, you will discover the Tree of Life. But be warned—it grows **upside down**, and its roots are invisible."

Aarav (confused): "How can a tree grow upside down?"

Krish Sir (smiling): "Because this is no ordinary tree. It's the world itself—full of branches of desires, roots of ego, and fruits of karma."

Allegory: The Tree = Material world. Roots = Source in divine. Branches = Our actions & desires. It grows downward = illusion.

Scene 2: "The Tree of Illusion" (Verses 3–6)

The students find a majestic **upside-down tree**, with shiny fruits and glittering leaves.

Sneha (excited): "Look! This fruit gives instant fame!"

Riya: "And this one gives lots of likes on social media!"

Suddenly, they see people stuck in the branches, tangled and lost.

Tree Guardian appears: "This tree will keep you climbing… but never free. Unless you cut it down with the sword of wisdom."

Metaphor: The Tree offers tempting fruits (desires) but traps you in the endless cycle of life (samsara).

Scene 3: "The Mirror of Truth" (Verses 7–10)

Mirror Fairy appears, holding a glowing mirror.

Mirror Fairy: "You've forgotten your true form. Look here!"

Aarav looks and sees a light glowing inside him.

Krish Sir: "That's your soul—eternal, pure, unchanging. The body changes, but *you* are beyond it."

Allegory: The mirror = Knowledge of self. The soul = divine spark. Most people are distracted and don't see it.

Scene 4: "Why Do We Forget?" (Verses 11–15)

Classmates get busy collecting magical fruits again.

Krish Sir: "Why do they forget? Because of attachment, pride, greed. The light is still inside them—but it's covered."

Sneha: "Can they remember?"

Krish Sir: "Yes. When they listen, think deeply, and see all life as connected to the Supreme Person."

Metaphor: Like a light covered with dust, the soul forgets its power due to worldly distractions.

Scene 5: "The Great Realization" (Verses 16–20)

The Tree starts shaking. The branches begin vanishing.

Tree Guardian: "The temporary world fades… but the eternal soul never dies."

Krish Sir (voice echoing): "There are two beings: the changing and the unchanging. But beyond both is **Puruṣottama**, the Supreme Soul."

Aarav: "So, I'm not the body, not even the mind. I'm a soul. And above me is the Supreme Soul."

Krish Sir: "Yes. He lives in your heart as a spark, guiding you when you're quiet and still."

Final Scene: "Back to the Classroom"

Everyone returns, changed.

Aarav: "Sir, I finally understand. The world is upside-down, but we can live upright—by remembering who we really are."

Krish Sir: "You have seen the truth. Now live with wisdom, serve with love, and keep your heart light."

Allegory & Metaphor Table – Chapter 15

Verse Range	Allegory / Story Element	Metaphor
15.1–2	Upside-down Tree	Material world, rooted in illusion, full of desires
15.3–6	Sword of Wisdom cuts tree	Knowledge removes attachment and ego
15.7–10	Mirror Fairy	True Self is soul; we forget due to illusion

15.11–15	Classmates distracted by fruit	Souls trapped by desires and ego
15.16–20	Light inside and Supreme Spark	Beyond body and soul is the Supreme Divine (Puruṣottama)

Kids' Insights & Takeaways

1. **The world seems attractive but is full of distractions.**
   Don't get stuck chasing shiny things.
2. **You are not your body or mind.**
   You are a soul—pure and divine.
3. **The Tree of Life grows upside-down.**
   What appears real may actually be illusion.
4. **Use wisdom like a sword.**
   Cut off your pride, laziness, and confusion.
5. **Puruṣottama lives in your heart.**
   Stay connected to that quiet inner voice.

Chapter 16

Title16: "The Two Seeds: The Tale of Aarav and Rudra"

Scene 1: The Gift of the Seeds

One sunny morning in a quiet village, Grandpa Krishna gathered his grandchildren—**Aarav** and **Rudra**—under the big mango tree.

"Today," Grandpa smiled, "I will give each of you a magical seed."

He opened his wooden box and pulled out **two seeds**—one **golden** and glowing faintly, the other **deep red** with fiery specks.

"These are no ordinary seeds," he said. "Each one holds a secret world. What grows depends on how you care for it."

Aarav chose the **golden seed**, while Rudra eagerly grabbed the **red one**.

Scene 2: Two Gardens Begin

Aarav found a quiet spot near a silent pond. He gently planted his seed, watered it every day, and even whispered kind words to it.

He also began helping others—sharing food with Anaya, feeding stray birds, and cleaning the courtyard without being asked.

Meanwhile, Rudra rushed to the corner of the backyard, dug a messy hole, and slammed the red seed into the ground.

He shouted at others, teased little Tara, and once yelled, **"Rules are stupid! I do what I want!"**

Scene 3: Gardens Reflect the Heart

Weeks passed. Aarav's garden began to **blossom**—beautiful golden leaves, calm breezes, butterflies dancing.

Rudra's garden, however, turned **thorny and wild**. The soil became dry, a strange **burning smell** rose, and dark clouds gathered above it.

One day, Rudra stomped back after losing a game and yelled, **"I deserve better! I'm stronger than all of you!"** His fists clenched with anger.

Grandpa Krishna gently placed his hand on Rudra's shoulder:
"Desire, anger, and greed... these are gates to sorrow, child. Beware the path you walk."

Scene 4: The Tale of Two Roads

That evening, Grandpa told them a story by the fire.

"There are two paths," he began. "One sunlit and peaceful, filled with trees and kind travelers. The other—stormy, with fire and howling winds. Every choice we make leads us down one of these roads."

Aarav listened quietly, thinking,
"I want to stay on the sunny road."

But Rudra just scoffed, **"There's no right or wrong. I make my own road."**

Scene 5: The Fall

One night, Rudra's garden **caught fire**. The wind howled, trees cracked, and Rudra found himself **lost in the smoke**, scared and confused.

"Help! Someone! I can't see!" he cried.

Suddenly, a soft light appeared—Aarav holding a lantern, his golden tree behind him shining bright.

Aarav reached out, “Come, Rudra. Let’s go back.”

Scene 6: The Realization

The next morning, Rudra sat beside Grandpa Krishna, tears rolling down his cheeks.

“Grandpa… I messed up. Can I… start again?”

Grandpa smiled warmly, holding out **another golden seed**.

“Every day is a chance to plant a new seed. What matters is what you choose next.”

Rudra hugged him and said, “This time… I’ll listen.”

Scene 7: A New Beginning

From that day on, Rudra began helping Anaya, apologized to Tara, and watered his new golden seed with care.

A few months later, **two blooming gardens** stood side by side—golden trees with soft fruits and peaceful air.

Grandpa Krishna whispered:
“The Deva and Asura seeds live in each of us. The one you water… grows.”

Moral of the Story:

"We all carry two seeds within us—the golden seed of goodness and the red seed of ego. What grows depends on our choices. Choose kindness, truth, and self-control, and your inner garden will bloom with joy and peace."

Allegory Table:

Bhagavad Gita Concept / Verse	Story Symbol / Scene	Allegorical Meaning
Deva & Asura seeds within us	Grandpa Krishna gives Aarav and Rudra each a seed: **Golden & Red**	Every person carries potential for both divine (good) and demoniac (bad) tendencies.
Daivi Sampat – Divine Qualities	Aarav planting the golden seed, helping others, speaking gently	Sattvic nature: truth, humility, compassion, discipline, non-violence. Leads to peace.
Asuri Sampat –	Rudra watering	Rajasic/Tamasic nature: ego,

Demoniac Qualities	the red seed, teasing others, acting with pride	anger, greed, harshness. Leads to suffering and downfall.
Inner World as a Garden	Aarav's garden blooming, Rudra's garden turning thorny	Our minds are like gardens. What qualities we feed (thoughts/actions) will grow.
Free Will / Choice	Aarav chooses to listen to Grandpa and reflect	We are not forced into one nature—we choose which path to follow with awareness.
Desire, Anger, Greed – Gates to Hell	Rudra clenching fists, yelling "I deserve more!"	These are inner enemies. If uncontrolled, they lead to sorrow, confusion, fear.
Ego and Arrogance	Rudra saying "I'm better than	False pride disconnects us from truth and invites conflict.

	everyone here!”	
Fearlessness in Goodness	Aarav standing up to Rudra kindly: “We don’t have to fight.”	True courage is peaceful. Sattvic nature doesn’t need to dominate—it uplifts quietly.
Result of Daivi Path	Aarav’s tree bearing golden fruit, peaceful aura	Divine behavior leads to inner joy, clarity, and positive influence on others.
Result of Asuri Path	Rudra’s tree burning from inside, stormy winds around	Demoniac behavior leads to fear, confusion, and eventual self-harm.
Guidance of the Shastra (Scriptures)	Grandpa Krishna’s stories and parables	Scriptures and wise mentors guide us when we're confused about right and wrong.

Final Realization & Redemption	Rudra finally crying, asking, "Can I plant again?"	Even one who followed the wrong path can change if they realize and choose rightly.

Summary Table for Students

Seed	Col or	Fed With	Grows Into	Leads To
Gold en Seed	Gol d	Kindne ss, truth, patienc e	Blossoming Tree (Daivi)	Joy, peace, harmon y
Red Seed	Red	Ego, anger, greed	Thorny/Bur ning Tree (Asuri)	Pain, fear, confusi on

Allegory Table:

Bhagavad Gita Concept / Verse	Symbol / Scene in Story	Allegorical Meaning
Daivi Sampat (Divine Qualities)	**Aarav, Anaya, kind**	Represent qualities like humility, truth, non-violence,

	helpers, silent pond	patience, self-control, fearlessness. These lead to inner peace and higher purpose.
Asuri Sampat (Demoniac Qualities)	**Rudra, Tara, wild bonfire, noisy crowd**	Symbolize arrogance, anger, harshness, selfishness, greed, pride, hypocrisy, and violence. These lead to downfall.
16.1–16.3: Divine traits	Aarav planting trees silently, sharing food	Shows non-egoistic, calm, kind actions – seeds of divine behavior.
16.4: Demoniac traits	Rudra shouting, throwing trash, bullying others	Represents ego, cruelty, ignorance, and destructive nature.
16.5: Two Paths – Liberation or Bondage	Grandpa Krishna's story of two roads	Divine qualities lead to freedom and growth, demoniac traits

	(sunlit vs stormy)	lead to suffering and fear.
16.7–16.9: Asuras deny dharma	Rudra mocks rules, says "There's no right or wrong!"	Asuras reject values, believe in chaos, no respect for truth or order.
16.10–16.12: Endless desires, greed	Tara hoarding all sweets, yelling "I want more!"	Describes selfish craving and fear of losing control, which causes pain.
16.13–16.15: Ego and Pride	Rudra brags: "I'm the best! I beat everyone!"	Ego blinds them. They believe they're always right and powerful.
16.16–16.20: Destiny of the Demoniac	Rudra lost in the forest fire, scared and crying	Shows the fall into confusion, fear, and suffering when divine nature is lost.
16.21–16.22: Three gates to hell	Grandpa Krishna shows 3 gates: **Desire, Anger, Greed**	These are the entry points to sorrow, like traps in the path of life.

16.23–16.24: Follow shastra and values	Aarav reading the “Book of Wisdom”	Shastra = inner compass. Right guidance leads to right action and safety.

Table for Students

Traits	Divine (Daivi Sampat)	Demoniac (Asuri Sampat)
Nature	Calm, honest, kind, humble	Proud, angry, selfish, violent
Speech	Truthful, soft, helpful words	Harsh, loud, boastful
Actions	Selfless, disciplined, helpful	Harmful, greedy, chaotic
Result	Peace, happiness, inner strength	Fear, pain, downfall
Example	Aarav, Anaya, Grandpa Krishna	Rudra, Tara

Moral Summary for Kids:

“Our thoughts, words, and actions build our path. If we act like heroes (Daivi), we grow strong and wise. If we act selfishly (Asuri), we lose our way. Always choose kindness, truth, and courage.”

Moral of the Story:

“We all carry two seeds within – Deva and Asura. The one we water grows. By choosing truth, kindness, and self-control, we walk the path of peace. By choosing pride, anger, and greed, we fall into sorrow. Always choose the golden seed.”

Chapter 16

Title16a: "The Light Within and the Shadow Game"

Theme:

This chapter talks about the **divine qualities (Daivi Sampat)** and **demonic qualities (Asuri Sampat)** inside every human being. It teaches us to recognize and nurture the good, and to be aware of and overcome the dark tendencies.

Characters:

- **Aarav** – The awakened soul-seeker
- **Sneha** – His wise little sister
- **Krish Sir** – The guiding teacher (like Krishna)
- **Shadow Lord (Asuro)** – The force representing ego, anger, pride
- **Light Fairy (Deviya)** – Represents kindness, truth, humility

- **Classmates** – Each pulled between good and bad choices

Scene 1: "The Two Scrolls" (Verse 1–3)

Setting: In class, Krish Sir brings two glowing scrolls—one blue, one black.

Krish Sir: "Children, today you will learn about the two types of powers within you—the **Divine** and the **Demonic**."

Sneha: "Are they like superheroes and villains?"

Krish Sir (smiling): "Something like that. But they both live… inside *you*."

Metaphor: The scrolls represent knowledge of qualities—truth vs. ignorance.

Scene 2: "Deviya and the Seeds of Goodness" (Verses 4–5)

In a dream, Aarav meets a glowing fairy—Deviya.

Deviya: "I plant seeds of truth, kindness, fearlessness, and patience."

Sneha: "What happens if we water these seeds?"

Deviya: "You grow into your highest self. You shine like the sun in the world."

Allegory: Divine qualities = Seeds of peace, truth, patience, etc.

Scene 3: "The Shadow Lord Appears" (Verses 6–9)

Suddenly, dark clouds swirl. A smoky figure appears—Shadow Lord Asuro.

Asuro (laughing): "Fear? Truth? Bah! Try anger, lies, and greed! Power is mine!"

He tempts the students with instant success, games, and trophies—but at the cost of hurting others.

Aarav: "But... what's the price?"

Asuro: "Just your peace. Just your joy. Nothing much." (evil laugh)

Metaphor: Demonic qualities = anger, deceit, selfishness, leading to destruction of inner peace.

Scene 4: "The Game of Choices" (Verses 10–13)

Students are divided. Some follow Deviya, others follow Asuro.

Krish Sir appears between them: "Children, every moment you're choosing. The Divine road is longer but leads to joy. The Demonic one is quick—but ends in darkness."

Classmate Riya: "What if we mix both?"

Krish Sir: "Even a drop of poison in pure water can destroy it."

Allegory: Life is a series of choices—small decisions lead to big consequences.

Scene 5: "The Fall and the Rise" (Verses 14–20)

Asuro tricks a few students. They cheat in a school competition and are caught. They feel ashamed.

Aarav (to them): "It's okay. You can change. We all have both seeds in us."

Krish Sir: "The one you feed will grow. Feed the Divine within you."

Deviya: "Don't fear. Just start again—with honesty, effort, and courage."

Moral: Mistakes can be corrected. Divine nature always welcomes us back.

Final Scene: "The Inner Battle"

Aarav holds the two scrolls.

Krish Sir: "You are the battlefield. And the winner is the one you feed."

Sneha: "So… every day is a new chance to choose the light?"

Krish Sir (smiling): "Yes, Sneha. That's true courage."

Allegory Table:

Verse Range	Allegory / Story Element	Metaphor
16.1–16.3	Two Scrolls of Light and Shadow	Divine and Demonic qualities in every human
16.4–16.5	Deviya planting seeds	Cultivating virtues (truth, kindness, fearlessness)
16.6–16.9	Shadow Lord tempting students	Ego, greed, and false pride leading to darkness
16.10–16.13	Game of Choices	Daily decisions shape our destiny
16.14–16.20	Cheating in competition	Wrong actions give short success but long regret

Kids' Insights & Takeaways

1. **You are not just good or bad—you are what you choose every day.**
   The Divine and the Demonic both live in you.
2. **Feed the good.**
   Be truthful, kind, patient, and fearless.
3. **Even if you make a mistake—you can restart.**
   What matters is learning from it.
4. **Peer pressure is a test.**
   Stay strong and choose your own light.
5. **Teachers and conscience guide us.**
   Listen closely to those who care.

Chapter 17

Title17: "The Three Lanterns: A Festival of Faith"

Characters:

- **Arjun** – A student invited to a festival in a magical village.
- **Grandpa Krishna** – His wise grandfather who helps him understand good and bad faith.
- **Red Lantern (Tamas)** – Lazy and confused in actions.
- **Grey Lantern (Rajas)** – Loud and proud, always chasing attention.
- **Golden Lantern (Sattva)** – Quiet, bright, and steady.
- **The Village of Shraddha** – A magical land where people live by their inner faith.

Scene 1: The Festival Invitation (Verse 1–3)

(Setting: Arjun finds a glowing invitation on his table. Grandpa Krishna enters.)

Arjun:
"Grandpa! Look! It's an invitation to the Festival of Faith in the Village of Shraddha!"

Grandpa Krishna (smiling):
"Ah, that's a place where people live by their inner beliefs. But remember, faith isn't always the same. There are three kinds – Sattvic (pure), Rajasic (passionate), and Tamasic (ignorant). Want to see how they look?"

(They enter the magical world together.)

Verse 1–3 talks about how everyone has faith based on their nature. Faith can be pure, passionate, or ignorant.

Scene 2: The Three Lanterns Appear (Verse 4–6)

(Three floating lanterns appear: one glowing gold (Sattva), one flashy silver-grey (Rajas), and one dull red (Tamas). Each calls Arjun.)

Red Lantern (grumbling):
"Follow me. Sit in the dark. No need to question. Just obey strange customs."

Grey Lantern (boasting):
"Join me in great sacrifices! Let the whole world see your greatness. It's all about the show!"

Golden Lantern (calmly):
"Come quietly. Let your heart offer light, not just the fire outside. No show, just sincerity."

Grandpa Krishna:
"See? Even sacrifice differs. Tamasic sacrifices are foolish. Rajasic ones are for show. But Sattvic sacrifices are done sincerely, without expecting rewards."

Verse 4–6 explains how even worship differs based on faith type—some worship ghosts (tamasic), some expect rewards (rajasic), and some serve selflessly (sattvic).

Scene 3: The Three Meals (Verse 7–10)

(Arjun sits at a grand dining hall. Three plates are brought to him:)

- **Sattvic Plate:** Fresh fruits, milk, and nourishing food.
- **Rajasic Plate:** Spicy chips, over-fried items, too much sugar.
- **Tamasic Plate:** Rotten leftovers and stale food.

Golden Lantern:
“Food that brings life, clarity, and health is Sattvic.”

Grey Lantern:
“This food is tasty and exciting, but it leaves you restless!”

Red Lantern:
“Heh. I don’t care. It’s food. Who needs freshness?”

Grandpa Krishna:
"Just like faith, even food shapes our mind. Choose wisely."

Verse 7–10 show how even food is of three kinds—Sattvic (healthy), Rajasic (exciting but unhealthy), and Tamasic (unfresh, dull, and harmful).

Scene 4: The Three Ways to Give (Verse 20–22)

(Arjun sees three people giving gifts at the festival fair.)

Sattvic Giver (quietly):
"I give this to help others. No need to mention my name."

Rajasic Giver (shouting):
"See what I donated?! Clap for me! I want recognition!"

Tamasic Giver (rudely):
"Take this and get lost! I don't even care who gets it!"

Grandpa Krishna:
"Giving with love and respect is Sattvic. Giving for fame is Rajasic. Giving without thought or care is Tamasic."

Verse 20–22 teaches the three types of charity based on the attitude behind the giving.

Scene 5: The Power of Words (Verse 14–19)

(Three people take turns speaking at the festival.)

Sattvic Speaker:
"Speak truth kindly. Never hurt others. Let your words heal."

Rajasic Speaker:
"Listen up, everyone! I'm the smartest! You all must obey me!"

Tamasic Speaker:
"Mumbling… cursing… gossiping."

Grandpa Krishna (to Arjun):
"Even speech and action can be Sattvic, Rajasic, or Tamasic. Always speak and act with kindness and clarity."

Verse 14–19 explain how our thoughts, speech, and discipline can be done in three ways – pure (Sattvic), showy (Rajasic), or dull and harsh (Tamasic).

Scene 6: The Magic Word – "Om Tat Sat" (Verse 23–28)

(At the end of the festival, the elder of Shraddha Village raises a glowing scroll.)

Elder:
"Let all who act with pure heart remember – '**Om Tat Sat**' – the three syllables of truth."

Golden Lantern:
"'Om' – for the Supreme. 'Tat' – for selfless work. 'Sat' – for truth, sincerity, and purity."

Grandpa Krishna:
"This is the seal of good action. Without faith and purity, even a good act loses meaning."

Arjun (nodding):
"I understand now, Grandpa. It's not about *what* I do, but *how* and *why* I do it."

Verse 23–28 explain the meaning of "Om Tat Sat" – the symbol of truth, dedication, and purity in all action.

Moral of the Story:

“Everything we do – eating, giving, speaking, or worshipping – should be done with the right intention. Sattvic faith is pure and brings peace. Choose it in your everyday life.”

Allegory Table:

Bhagavad Gita Verse/Concept	**Symbol in Story**	**Allegorical Meaning**
17.1–17.3: Three types of faith	Three lanterns (Golden, Grey, Red)	**Sattva** (pure): Golden lantern, **Rajas** (passionate): Grey lantern, **Tamas** (ignorant): Red lantern. Each reflects different mindsets.
17.4–17.6: Types of Worship	Each lantern calling Arjun with their	Sattvic worships selflessly, Rajasic worships for show, Tamasic

	worship style	worships blindly or harmfully.
17.7–17.10: Types of Food	Three food plates – fresh (Sattvic), spicy (Rajasic), stale (Tamasic)	Food also affects mind and body; pure food nourishes both, while impure food harms.
17.14–17.16: Tapas (Austerity) of Body, Speech, and Mind	Three speakers at the festival	Sattvic: gentle, kind speech. Rajasic: arrogant. Tamasic: hurtful or meaningless.
17.17–17.19: Tapas with faith, show, or foolishness	Intent behind behavior of lanterns	Discipline done with sincerity is Sattvic; for show is Rajasic; with confusion or harm is Tamasic.
17.20–17.22: Three types of charity	Gift-givers at the festival fair	Giving with love and no expectation (Sattvic), with pride (Rajasic),

		or carelessly (Tamasic).
17.23–17.28: Om Tat Sat – Symbol of True Action	Magic scroll and elder's speech about "Om Tat Sat"	These three words symbolize pure intention in action—acting for God, selflessness, and truth.

Summary for Students:

Faith Type	Color	Behavior	Food	Speech	Giving Style
Sattvic	Gold	Calm, wise	Fresh & clean	Kind, healing words	Quiet, humble, thoughtful
Rajasic	Grey	Showy, proud	Spicy, too rich	Loud, bragging	For name and fame
Tamasic	Red	Lazy, confused	Rotten, stale	Harsh, hurtful	Careless, harmful

Chapter 17

Title17a: "The Festival of Faith"

Theme:

This chapter explores the **three types of faith (Shraddha)—Sattvic (pure)**, **Rajasic (passionate)**, and **Tamasic (ignorant)**—and how our faith shapes our thoughts, actions, food, speech, and even charity.

Characters:

Aarav – The soul-searching boy

- **Sneha** – His smart sister
- **Krish Sir** – The wise teacher (like Krishna)
- **Tanu** – Focused, calm student (Sattvic)
- **Ravi** – Ambitious, wants praise (Rajasic)
- **Bunty** – Lazy and confused (Tamasic)
- **Principal Aunty** – Organizer of the Faith Festival

Scene 1: "The Faith Festival" (Verses 1–3)

Setting: The school is preparing for a grand "Festival of Faith." Principal Aunty explains:

Principal: "Students, your stalls and events will reflect your true **faith**. You may not even realize it, but faith guides your food, actions, prayers, and intentions."

Krish Sir (whispering to Aarav): "Let's watch carefully. You'll see three paths forming."

Metaphor: Festival = Life's choices; Each student = different kind of faith (Sattvic, Rajasic, Tamasic)

Scene 2: "Three Students, Three Stalls" (Verses 4–6)

- **Tanu's Stall:** A peaceful meditation corner. She helps others calm their minds.
- **Ravi's Stall:** Flashy banners, prizes, selfie-booth. He constantly announces: "Come here! Best stall ever!"
- **Bunty's Stall:** Dark, weird symbols, messy setup. He mumbles: "I just did what some YouTube guy said…"

Sneha (to Aarav): "Wow, they all pray or believe in *something*, but so differently!"

Krish Sir: "Exactly. All have Shraddha. But what kind?"

Allegory: Each stall = reflection of inner faith.
Sattvic = peace and truth.
Rajasic = pride and reward.
Tamasic = confusion and superstition.

Scene 3: "Food for the Soul" (Verses 7–10)

During lunch break, three types of food are served:

- **Tanu's choice:** Fresh fruits, light and nourishing meals.
- **Ravi's pick:** Spicy fried food, full of taste and drama.
- **Bunty's meal:** Old snacks, stale chips, weird mix of sweets and chips.

Krish Sir: "Even food affects your mind. What you eat is what you become."

Metaphor:

- Sattvic = Clean, energizing food
- Rajasic = Overly spicy, pleasure-driven
- Tamasic = Spoiled, dull, harmful

Scene 4: "Words of Faith" (Verses 11–13)

Each student presents a talk:

- **Tanu:** Calmly explains helping others without expecting anything.
- **Ravi:** Talks big but secretly expects a trophy.
- **Bunty:** Doesn't prepare, blames the system.

Krish Sir: "Kids, even rituals must be done with the right intent."

Allegory:

- Sattvic = done selflessly
- Rajasic = done for praise
- Tamasic = done carelessly or without purpose

Scene 5: "The Charity Box" (Verses 20–22)

All students drop money in the school charity box.

- **Tanu:** Quietly gives without anyone knowing.
- **Ravi:** Announces, "I'm donating ₹500!" and expects applause.
- **Bunty:** Grumbles, "I guess I have to…" and throws a coin lazily.

Krish Sir: "The gift is not the money. It's the *heart* behind it."

Metaphor: True charity = done quietly, timely, to the right cause.

Scene 6: "The Magic of Om-Tat-Sat" (Verses 23–28)

Krish Sir explains a secret mantra behind all actions:

- **Om** – Begin with respect
- **Tat** – Done without ego
- **Sat** – Do it truthfully and purely

He teaches the class to chant before starting any task.

Aarav: "So... even our *faith festival* was a mirror of our inner world?"

Krish Sir: "Yes, Aarav. And now you know how to clean your mirror."

Allegory & Metaphor Table – Chapter 17

Verse Range	Allegory / Story Element	Metaphor
17.1–17.3	The Faith Festival	Types of faith (Sattvic, Rajasic, Tamasic) guide actions
17.4–17.6	Student stalls	Worship styles reflect personality and intention

17.7–17.10	Three types of lunch	Food affects your faith and mind
17.11–17.13	Speeches during the event	Rituals must be done selflessly, not for reward
17.20–17.22	Charity Box donations	Giving reveals purity of heart
17.23–17.28	Om-Tat-Sat mantra lesson	Every pure act begins with awareness, humility, and truth

Kids' Insights & Takeaways

1. **Faith is not only about praying—it's in your actions, food, words, and giving.**
2. **There are three kinds of faith—pure, proud, and careless.**
3. **What you believe becomes how you behave.**
4. **The real magic lies in doing things with respect, selflessness, and truth.**
5. **Choose to become like Tanu—peaceful and purposeful—not like Bunty or Ravi lost in praise or laziness.**

TANU

Chapter 18

Title18: "The Last Challenge: Aarav's Choice of the Crown"

Main Characters:

- **Aarav** – the thoughtful student-hero who seeks truth and freedom
- **Rudra** – his ambitious but prideful friend
- **Grandpa Krishna** – the wise storyteller and guide
- **Tara** – a curious and kind girl who supports Aarav
- **The Three Crowns** – Gold, Silver, and Iron: symbols of different gunas (qualities)

Scene 1: The Kingdom of Karma

[Setting: A mystical school where students graduate by choosing one of three crowns representing their destiny.]

Grandpa Krishna: “Today is your final challenge, children. In this land of Karma, each action counts. But it is not just *what* you do—it’s *how* and *why* you do it.”

Tara: “Grandpa, we’re all nervous. There are three crowns—how do we know which one leads to happiness?”

Grandpa Krishna: “Each crown represents your inner quality—Sattva, Rajas, or Tamas. Let me tell you a story…”

Verse 1–12: Renunciation & Right Action

[Flashback begins: Aarav dreams of three travelers—Sage (Sattvic), Warrior (Rajasic), and Sleeper (Tamasic).]

- The **Sage** gives up attachment, works for the good of all. “I do my duty, expecting nothing.”
- The **Warrior** seeks rewards. “I fight to win fame and praise.”
- The **Sleeper** avoids duty. “Why work? It’s too hard.”

→ **Metaphor**: True renunciation is not leaving work, but giving up attachment and ego.

Aarav (to himself): “I want to be like the Sage—free yet responsible.”

Verse 13–18: The Five Factors of Action

Grandpa Krishna: "Every action has five causes: the doer, the body, the tools, the effort, and fate. Understand this before you blame or boast."

Scene: Aarav works on a science project. Tara helps, Rudra interrupts.

Rudra: "I did it all! I'm the best!"

Tara: "But Aarav planned it, I helped build it… and don't forget, even the weather helped dry the paint!"

Lesson: Success is teamwork—inner and outer forces work together.

Verse 23–28: The Three Types of Action

- **Sattvic Action**: Done with no selfish aim, calm and steady.
  → Aarav helps clean the garden without expecting praise.
- **Rajasic Action**: Done for reward, with pride.
  → Rudra joins only when cameras arrive.
- **Tamasic Action**: Done in confusion or harmfully.
  → A classmate tramples plants, not caring.

Moral: The intention behind action matters more than the action itself.

Verse 29–35: The Three Types of Understanding

Grandpa Krishna places 3 lenses before them.

- **Sattvic Lens** – Sees clearly: good as good, bad as bad.
- **Rajasic Lens** – Sees only profit and loss.
- **Tamasic Lens** – Sees truth as false, and false as truth.

Tara: "Through the Sattvic lens, I can see right and wrong so clearly!"

Metaphor: Our *intellect* is the lens we use to judge. Sharpen it with truth.

Verse 36–40: Three Kinds of Happiness

- **Sattvic Joy**: Hard at first, peaceful later.
→ Studying, practicing, learning.
- **Rajasic Joy**: Sweet at first, bitter later.
→ Junk food, distractions.
- **Tamasic Joy**: Delusion and laziness from the start.
→ Sleeping through class.

Aarav: "True joy takes effort—but lasts forever."

Moral: Choose lasting happiness over quick pleasure.

Final Scene: The Three Crowns

Grandpa Krishna: "Now choose your crown."

- **Rudra runs to the Golden Crown**, which glows bright. "It's the most expensive—mine!"
- **Tara admires the Silver Crown** with flowers and gems.
- **Aarav steps back**, remembers all the lessons.

Aarav: "I choose none—not for glory, but for truth. I'll serve without pride, walk the path of duty."

A hidden door opens behind the crowns. A light shines.

Grandpa Krishna smiles: "That is Moksha—the door to freedom. You renounced pride, saw clearly, and acted with faith. You win the true crown."

Moral of the Story:

"True freedom comes not from giving up work, but from giving up ego. Right action with clear understanding and selfless purpose leads to lasting happiness."

Allegory Table:

Bhagavad Gita Verse / Concept	Story Scene / Symbol	Allegorical Meaning for Students
17.1–17.3: Sannyasa & Tyaga (Renunciation & Relinquishment)	Grandpa Krishna gives challenge to “choose the right crown”	Real renunciation is not quitting duties, but giving up ego, selfish desires, and attachment.
17.4–17.12: True renunciation is mental, not physical	Aarav remember s Sage, Warrior, and Sleeper travelers	Giving up action isn't renunciation —doing duty with no pride is.
17.13–17.17: Five causes of action	Science project scene: effort by Aarav, tools, help from Tara, time, fate	Actions have many factors—don’t boast or blame. Work humbly and share credit.
17.18–17.22: Knowledge types (Sattvic,	Grandpa Krishna gives three books:	See clearly: Knowledge should unite, not divide or

Rajasic, Tamasic)	clear (truth), confusing (profit), and false (delusion)	create confusion.
17.23–17.28: Types of action (Sattvic, Rajasic, Tamasic)	Aarav helps garden quietly (Sattvic); Rudra poses for camera (Rajasic); classmate destroys plants (Tamasic)	The same act can be noble or selfish depending on motive.
17.29–17.35: Intellect and resolve (buddhi & dhriti)	Three magic lenses—Aarav sees truth clearly, Rudra only gain, and classmate sees good as bad	We must train our understandin g to choose right over easy.

17.36–17.40: Types of happiness	Junk food vs. studying; Aarav chooses discipline	Sattvic joy is long-lasting but slow; Rajasic joy fades; Tamasic joy is harmful.
17.41–17.48: Duties by nature	Grandpa says: "You must act as per your nature"	Everyone has their dharma. Better to follow your path imperfectly than another's perfectly.
17.49–17.55: Renouncing ego leads to peace	Aarav lets go of praise and simply does his duty	Letting go of pride and doership leads to peace and wisdom.
17.56–17.66: Surrender to the Divine	Aarav surrenders to the light behind the crowns	Trusting the divine and doing your best opens the door to true joy and moksha (freedom).

17.67–17.78: Final words & blessings	Grandpa Krishna blesses Aarav: “You understood the deepest truth.”	Those who follow truth selflessly are beloved and protected.

Character Mapping:

Bhagavad Gita Element	Story Character / Symbol	Representation
Krishna (Teacher/Guide)	Grandpa Krishna	The divine teacher guiding with wisdom and clarity
Arjuna (Seeker)	Aarav	The student facing moral and life dilemmas
Maya / Illusion	The shiny crowns	False temptations and distractions of reward and glory
Gita’s Teachings	Magical lenses, 3 books	Tools to understand

		right from wrong
Ego / Pride	Rudra	Desires control, recognition, and reward
Dharma	Garden-cleaning, project work	Doing one's duty without selfish expectation

Summary Table for Young Learners

Crown	**Symbolizes**	**What Happens**
Gold Crown	Glory, fame, ego (Rajasic)	Rudra runs after it, but it leads nowhere
Silver Crown	Pleasing, comfort (Tamasic)	Tara admires it but doesn't choose
Invisible Door	True wisdom (Sattvic)	Aarav chooses truth, enters a secret path of peace and joy

Final Moral for Students:

"You are free when you stop acting for applause, and start acting from love and clarity. Do your duty without pride, see clearly, and you will walk the path of freedom."

Chapter 18

Title18a: "The Final Choice"

A journey ends. A new world begins.

Characters:

- **Aarav** – The soul-searching boy
- **Sneha** – His kind and clever sister
- **Krish Sir** – The wise teacher (Krishna figure)
- **Principal Aunty** – Represents life's higher authority
- **Tanu, Ravi, Bunty** – Represent Sattvic, Rajasic, Tamasic natures respectively
- **Schoolmates, Teachers, Parents** – Society, world, karma

Scene 1: "The Graduation Test" (Verses 1–12)

Setting: The last day of school. All students will now receive their "Life Compass" — a final test to choose **Action or Renunciation**.

Principal Aunty: "Some think giving up action leads to peace. Others say wise action brings growth. Who is right?"

Aarav (turns to Krish Sir): "Do I fight for change or just let go of everything?"

Krish Sir: "True renunciation is not about leaving work. It's leaving the ego behind while doing the work."

Allegory:

- Life Compass = Dharma
- Renunciation = Giving up ego, not duty

Scene 2: "The Tree of Choices" (Verses 13–18)

Krish Sir takes the students under a giant tree.

Krish Sir: "Every action has **5 elements**:

1. The doer
2. The action
3. The tools
4. The effort
5. The divine will behind it."

He hands out leaves from the tree. Aarav's leaf says: *"You are not the leaf, you are the wind that flows through it."*

Metaphor: Life = Tree of actions. We act, but the outcome flows through higher forces.

Scene 3: "The Performer's Play" (Verses 23–40)

Students perform a play. Krish Sir narrates as they act:

- **Sattvic worker (Tanu):** Calm, steady, does her part happily.
- **Rajasic worker (Ravi):** Overdoes, seeks applause.
- **Tamasic worker (Bunty):** Complains, skips scenes.

Krish Sir: "Each performer lives in a guna (quality). Learn to act in harmony, not for reward."

Allegory:

- Life = A play
- Gunas = Modes of being that color your performance

Scene 4: "What's Your Duty?" (Verses 41–49)

Principal Aunty: "Every child has a strength. Don't copy others. Do your **Svadharma**."

Aarav realizes he loves teaching and wants to guide kids.

Aarav: "Even if I'm not perfect, I must follow my true role."

Metaphor:

- Svadharma = Inner compass
- Don't become someone else's shadow—shine your own light

Scene 5: "The Surrender" (Verses 50–66)

In a final meeting, Aarav is confused.

Aarav: "Sir, I've learned so much. But still... how do I become free?"

Krish Sir (softly): "Drop your pride. Surrender your actions to the Divine. Let go, and *you shall rise*."

Suddenly, the stage glows. All students kneel as Krish Sir's form shines brilliantly like light flowing through everyone.

Krish Sir (with glowing aura):
"Abandon all doubts. Surrender to Me. I shall carry you across the sea of sorrow."

Allegory:

- Liberation = Surrender of ego, not duty
- Krish Sir = Divine wisdom in every heart

- Moksha = Freedom through wisdom and humility

Scene 6: "The Final Bell" (Verses 67–78)

Sneha hugs Aarav: "You did it, brother!"

Aarav smiles: "No, we all did. The Gita wasn't just a lesson—it's a map of our own mind."

The final bell rings. The students walk toward the sun, a new life ahead.

Allegory Table:

Verse Range	Story Element	Allegory / Metaphor
18.1–18.12	Graduation Test	Renunciation is giving up ego, not duty
18.13–18.18	Tree of Choices	5 causes of action = nature, tools, doer, effort, divine will
18.23–18.40	The Performer's Play	3 Gunas = modes of working
18.41–18.49	"Find Your Duty"	Svadharma = Inner compass, true calling
18.50–18.66	Aarav's Surrender	Liberation through surrender
18.67–18.78	The Final Bell	Divine wisdom is the final guide

Kids' Takeaways & Final Insights

1. **You don't have to escape life to be free—you must let go of ego.**
2. **Every action has many parts. Do your best, but accept outcomes gracefully.**
3. **You are unique—follow your inner gift, not someone else's dream.**
4. **Real surrender is trusting life and being your truest self.**
5. **The Gita is not a book outside—it's the story within you.**

Moral of the Entire Journey (Chapters 1–18)

"When you know who you truly are, act without pride, and trust the divine flow—you become unstoppable, peaceful, and free."

RENUNCIATION
IS GIVING UP EGO, NOT DUTY

The Gita is not a book
outside - it's the
story within you.

INDEX

Chapter 1: Arjuna Vishada Yoga (The Yoga of Arjuna's Dejection)

Gist: *Despair leads to self-inquiry.*
Insight: Even a great warrior like Arjuna can feel lost. Confusion is often the starting point of deep wisdom.

Chapter 2: Sankhya Yoga (Transcendental Knowledge)

Gist: *Know the eternal Self.*
Insight: The soul is immortal. Detachment and duty go hand-in-hand. Begin your journey with self-awareness and purpose.

Chapter 3: Karma Yoga (Path of Selfless Action)

Gist: *Act without attachment.*
Insight: Perform your duty without craving results. Right action purifies the mind.

Chapter 4: Jnana Karma Sanyasa Yoga (Wisdom in Action)

Gist: *Blend wisdom with action.*
Insight: Action done with awareness becomes

worship. Knowledge transforms work into spiritual growth.

Chapter 5: Karma Sanyasa Yoga (Renunciation vs. Action)

Gist: *Inner renunciation matters more.*
Insight: True renunciation is mental detachment, not escape. Be in the world, but not of it.

Chapter 6: Dhyana Yoga (The Yoga of Meditation)

Gist: *Discipline your mind through meditation.*
Insight: A calm, focused mind is your greatest tool. The true yogi sees all beings as one.

Chapter 7: Jnana Vijnana Yoga (Knowledge & Realization)

Gist: *Know Me fully – both form and formless.*
Insight: Understanding God involves both material and spiritual aspects. Faith opens the door to divine knowledge.

Chapter 8: Akshara Brahma Yoga (The Imperishable Supreme)

Gist: *Remember the divine at all times.*
Insight: Your final thoughts shape your next

journey. Constant remembrance leads to liberation.

Chapter 9: Raja Vidya Raja Guhya Yoga (King of Knowledge & Secrets)

Gist: *God is both beyond and within.*
Insight: The divine loves all equally. Even the worst sinner can be uplifted by devotion.

Chapter 10: Vibhuti Yoga (Divine Glories)

Gist: *See divinity in everything.*
Insight: Every great quality or power is a spark of Krishna's infinite glory.

Chapter 11: Vishwarupa Darshana Yoga (Vision of the Universal Form)

Gist: *The One is all; all is One.*
Insight: Realizing the vastness of the divine inspires awe and surrender.

Chapter 12: Bhakti Yoga (Path of Devotion)

Gist: *Love is the highest path.*
Insight: Simple, heartfelt devotion transcends ritual and philosophy. God responds to pure love.

Chapter 13: Kshetra Kshetrajna Vibhaga Yoga (Field & Knower of the Field)

Gist: *Know the difference between body and soul.*
Insight: The body is the field; the soul is the knower. Wisdom begins with self-inquiry.

Chapter 14: Gunatraya Vibhaga Yoga (Three Modes of Nature)

Gist: *Rise above the three gunas.*
Insight: Sattva, Rajas, and Tamas bind the soul. Transcend them to reach liberation.

Chapter 15: Purushottama Yoga (The Supreme Person)

Gist: *Detach from the world tree; seek the root.*
Insight: The world is like an upside-down tree. Cut attachment and find your way back to the source — the Supreme.

Chapter 16: Daivasura Sampad Vibhaga Yoga (Divine & Demonic Natures)

Gist: *Cultivate divine qualities.*
Insight: Humility, non-violence, truthfulness lead to liberation. Ego, anger, greed lead to bondage.

Chapter 17: Shraddhatraya Vibhaga Yoga (Threefold Faith)

Gist: *Your faith shapes your destiny.*
Insight: Even faith and sacrifice are influenced by the gunas. Choose the path of clarity and harmony.

Chapter 18: Moksha Sanyasa Yoga (Liberation through Renunciation)

Gist: *Let go, and be free.*
Insight: Real freedom comes through inner renunciation, right action, and surrender to the Divine.

Main Characters of the Mahabharata

Group	Characters	Description
Pandavas	Yudhishthira, Bhima, Arjuna, Nakula, Sahadeva	Sons of King Pandu. Heroes of the story.
Kauravas	Duryodhana, Dushasana, and 98 brothers	Cousins of the Pandavas; led by Duryodhana.
Krishna	Lord and guide to the Pandavas	Avatar of Vishnu; Arjuna's charioteer and spiritual guide.
Draupadi	Wife of all five Pandavas	Princess of Panchala, brave and wise.
Bhishma	Grandsire of both Pandavas & Kauravas	Wise elder who took a vow of celibacy.

Drona	Guru of both families	Master of warfare and weaponry.
Karna	Friend of Duryodhana	Secretly the eldest son of Kunti (Pandavas' mother).
Shakuni	Uncle of Kauravas	Mastermind behind the dice game and many tricks.
Dhritarashtra	Blind king of Hastinapura	Father of the Kauravas.
Kunti	Mother of the Pandavas	Wise and devoted mother.
Vidura	Wise counselor	Always stands for justice and dharma.

Mahabharata - Story

1. Adi Parva – *The Beginning*

Story: Tells the origin of the Kuru family, birth of Pandavas and Kauravas, and how the Pandavas marry Draupadi.

- King Shantanu marries Ganga and then Satyavati.
- Bhishma takes a vow never to marry.
- Pandu and Dhritarashtra are born.
- Pandu has five sons (Pandavas), and Dhritarashtra has 100 sons (Kauravas).
- Pandavas and Kauravas learn from Guru Drona.
- Arjuna wins Draupadi in a swayamvara.
- Pandavas build Indraprastha and rule it.

Insight: Every great story begins with choices—good or bad.
Moral: Character matters more than birth.

✅ **Right:** Keeping promises (Bhishma), learning and using knowledge wisely (Pandavas).

❌ **Wrong:** Jealousy (Kauravas), unfair favoritism (Dhritarashtra).

Moral: *A strong start comes from truth, values, and learning.*

2. Sabha Parva – *The Dice Game*

Story: Yudhishthira loses his kingdom and Draupadi in a dice game. Draupadi is insulted, but Krishna saves her.

- Yudhishthira is invited to a dice game by Duryodhana.
- He loses his kingdom, wealth, brothers, and Draupadi.
- Draupadi is insulted in the court.
- Krishna saves Draupadi.
- Pandavas are sent into 13 years of exile.

Insight: Even heroes fall when they forget what is right.
Moral: Never gamble with your future.

✅ Right: Standing up for yourself with dignity (Draupadi).

❌ Wrong: Gambling, insulting women, remaining silent in injustice.

Moral: Never risk what you love for pride or greed.

3. Vana Parva – *The Forest Life*

Story: The Pandavas live in exile for 13 years. They learn, grow, and prepare for the future.

- Pandavas live in the forest.
- They meet sages, learn lessons, and grow wiser.
- Arjuna goes to heaven to get divine weapons.
- Draupadi is kidnapped but saved by Bhima.
- Many adventures and spiritual teachings happen.

Insight: Hard times are lessons in disguise.
Moral: Growth happens in silence and struggle.

✅ **Right:** Patience, learning from nature and sages, humility.

❌ **Wrong:** Seeking revenge during a time meant for reflection.

Moral: *Difficult times are meant for growth, not revenge.*

4. Virata Parva – *The Hidden Year*

Story: Pandavas live in disguise in King Virata's palace. Arjuna teaches dance as Brihannala!

- Pandavas spend their 13th year in disguise.
- They serve in King Virata's court secretly.
- Arjuna becomes a dance teacher named Brihannala.
- At the end, they reveal their identity after a war with the Kauravas.

Insight: True strength is quiet and clever.
Moral: Be humble; real strength doesn't show off.

✅ Right: Staying true to duty even in disguise, protecting others.

❌ Wrong: Underestimating others based on appearances.

Moral: True strength stays strong even in hiding.

---

5. Udyoga Parva – *The Preparation for War*

Story: Krishna tries for peace, but Duryodhana refuses. War becomes unavoidable.

- Both sides prepare for war.
- Krishna offers peace, but Duryodhana refuses.
- Krishna gives the choice—his army or himself. Arjuna chooses Krishna.
- War becomes certain.

Insight: Peace must be chosen before it's lost.
Moral: Ego can destroy everything.

✅ Right: Trying for peace, honesty, choosing Krishna over weapons.

❌ Wrong: Pride, ego, rejecting good advice (Duryodhana).

Moral: A wise heart chooses peace over pride.

---

6. Bhishma Parva – *The Battle Begins*

Story: First 10 days of war under Bhishma's command. Arjuna receives the Bhagavad Gita from Krishna.

- The great Kurukshetra war begins.
- Krishna gives Arjuna the **Bhagavad Gita**.
- Arjuna is confused about fighting his family.
- Krishna explains duty and dharma.
- Bhishma leads the Kaurava army for 10 days.

- Bhishma is finally defeated by Arjuna using Shikhandi.

Insight: Even war needs wisdom.
Moral: Do your duty with a pure heart.

✅ Right: Doing one's duty with courage (Arjuna), guiding with truth (Krishna).

❌ Wrong: Fighting with hatred or ego.

Moral: True warriors fight for justice, not hatred.

---

7. Drona Parva – *The Mighty Guru Fights*

Story: Drona becomes commander. Many heroes die, including Abhimanyu.

- Drona becomes the commander.
- Fierce battles take place.
- Abhimanyu (Arjuna's son) enters the Chakravyuha and is killed.
- Drona is tricked and killed by Dhrishtadyumna.

Insight: Knowledge without kindness can be dangerous.
Moral: Use your skills for good.

✅ **Right:** Protecting others even in war, fighting fairly.

❌ **Wrong:** Using trickery to win, taking life without cause (Abhimanyu's death).

Moral: *No victory is great if it causes innocent suffering.*

8. Karna Parva – *Karna vs Arjuna*

Story: Karna leads the Kaurava army. He fights bravely but dies in battle.

- Karna becomes the commander.
- He fights bravely and almost defeats Arjuna.
- Krishna saves Arjuna at key moments.
- Karna's chariot wheel gets stuck, and Arjuna kills him.

Insight: Loyalty must be toward truth.
Moral: Knowing right and still doing wrong is dangerous.

✅ **Right:** Loyalty, bravery, keeping promises (Karna).

❌ **Wrong:** Supporting the wrong side knowingly, pride over truth.

Moral: *Bravery is not enough—righteousness matters more.*

9. Shalya Parva – *Final Clash*

Story: Shalya leads the Kaurava army. Duryodhana is defeated by Bhima.

- Shalya becomes commander.
- Duryodhana fights Bhima with a mace.
- Bhima hits Duryodhana below the waist and defeats him.

Insight: Pride always leads to fall.
Moral: Choose humility over ego.

✅ **Right:** Finishing conflict to restore peace.

❌ **Wrong:** Fighting with anger and hatred till the end.

Moral: *Win with honor, not with hatred.*

---

10. Sauptika Parva – *The Night Attack*

Story: Ashwatthama attacks the Pandava camp at night, killing innocent sons.

- Ashwatthama, son of Drona, attacks at night.
- He kills the sleeping sons of the Pandavas.
- The war is over, but sorrow remains.

Insight: Revenge harms the soul.
Moral: Even victory without values is hollow.

✅ **Right:** Forgiveness, self-control in pain.

❌ **Wrong:** Revenge, killing the innocent during sleep (Ashwatthama).

Moral: *Revenge causes more darkness, not justice.*

---

11. Stri Parva – *The Women Mourn*

Story: The women of both sides cry for their lost loved ones.

- The women of Hastinapura mourn their lost husbands and sons.
- Gandhari curses Krishna, foretelling the destruction of his Yadava clan.

Insight: War hurts all, not just fighters.
Moral: Violence breaks many hearts.

✅ **Right:** Grieving with dignity, learning from mistakes.

❌ **Wrong:** Ignoring the pain war causes to families.

Moral: *War may end, but its wounds remain.*

12. Shanti Parva – *Peace Talks*

Story: Yudhishthira becomes king but is sad. Bhishma, on his deathbed, teaches about dharma.

- Yudhishthira becomes king but feels sad.
- Bhishma, on his deathbed, teaches about duty, kingship, and life.
- Yudhishthira begins to heal.

Insight: Wisdom shines brightest in silence.
Moral: A wise king listens more than he speaks.

☑ **Right:** Listening to wise elders, ruling with peace.

✖ **Wrong:** Letting guilt freeze you from action.

Moral: *A true leader learns before leading.*

13. Anushasana Parva – *Instructions of Wisdom*

Story: Bhishma gives final instructions before dying. Talks about charity, truth, and duty.

- Bhishma continues teaching about morals, charity, respect, and dharma.

- Then Bhishma dies peacefully on the bed of arrows.

Insight: Last words often carry the most truth.
Moral: Serve others with love.

✅ **Right:** Charity, honesty, caring for others.

❌ **Wrong:** Using power for selfishness.

Moral: *Kindness and discipline make life meaningful.*

---

14. Ashwamedha Parva – *The Horse Sacrifice*

Story: Yudhishthira performs a grand sacrifice to restore dharma. Arjuna follows the horse across lands.

- Yudhishthira performs a horse sacrifice to prove his right to rule.
- Arjuna follows the horse across many kingdoms and wins back support.

Insight: Leadership means restoring balance.
Moral: Goodness spreads when you take action.

✅ **Right:** Winning hearts, restoring peace, ruling justly.

❌ **Wrong:** Pride in conquest without purpose.

Moral: *Rule through service, not through fear.*

---

15. Ashramavasika Parva – *The Forest Life of Elders*

Story: Dhritarashtra, Gandhari, and Kunti leave for the forest and live a peaceful life.

- Dhritarashtra, Gandhari, and Kunti go to the forest.
- They spend their final days in prayer and meditation.
- They die in a forest fire peacefully.

Insight: Peace follows surrender.
Moral: Forgiveness is freedom.

✅ **Right:** Letting go of attachment, finding peace in nature.

❌ **Wrong:** Holding onto anger or sorrow forever.

Moral: *True wisdom is learning when to step away.*

---

16. Mausala Parva – *The End of Yadavas*

Story: Krishna's clan destroys itself. Krishna leaves his body.

- Krishna's clan, the Yadavas, fight among themselves and destroy each other.
- Krishna is killed by a hunter's arrow.
- Balarama also leaves his body.

Insight: Everything has an end—even great dynasties.
Moral: Pride in power brings downfall.

✅ **Right:** Fulfilling destiny, accepting endings.

❌ **Wrong:** Pride in power, ignoring warnings (Yadavas).

Moral: *Even the greatest fall when arrogance grows.*

17. Mahaprasthanika Parva – *The Great Journey*

Story: Pandavas renounce the kingdom and walk to the Himalayas. Only Yudhishthira reaches the end.

- The Pandavas renounce the kingdom and walk to the Himalayas.

- One by one, they fall, only Yudhishthira reaches the top.
- A dog follows him—it's Dharma in disguise.

Insight: Truth walks alone but always reaches the top.
Moral: Dharma leads you to the highest.

✅ **Right:** Walking the path of truth till the end.

❌ **Wrong:** Giving up dharma for comfort or pride.

Moral: *In the end, only truth walks with you.*

---

18. Swargarohanika Parva – *The Climb to Heaven*

Story: Yudhishthira goes to heaven and sees both friends and enemies. Finally, he finds peace.

- Yudhishthira, the eldest Pandava, starts his final journey to heaven.
- All his brothers and Draupadi fall one by one during the journey.
- A loyal **dog** walks with Yudhishthira till the very end.
- A divine chariot appears to take Yudhishthira to heaven.

- He is **asked to leave the dog behind**.
- He **refuses**, saying he won't abandon one who stayed loyal.
- It turns out the dog is **Dharma (the god of righteousness)** in disguise.
- In heaven, Yudhishthira is first shown his enemies enjoying luxuries and his brothers in hell.
- He chooses to **stay with his brothers**, even in hell.
- The gods reveal it was a test—and reward him with the **real heaven**.

Insight: Heaven is for those who hold on to truth till the end.
Moral: Truth and kindness always win.

✅ **Right:** Loyalty to goodness, love for truth.

- **Loyalty to good:** Yudhishthira stays loyal to the dog (which stands for goodness and truth), even when tempted by heaven.
- **Love for truth:** He doesn't care about reward or appearances—he sticks to what's *right*, even if it means sacrifice.

- **Compassion:** He won't leave behind a loyal friend for personal gain.
- **Choosing values over comfort.**

✕ **Wrong:** Judging only by appearances.

- **Judging by appearances:** Heaven and hell were shown differently, but they were illusions—a test of judgment.
- **Abandoning what is right for rewards:** Choosing reward and comfort over truth would have been a failure.
- **Thinking success means being in heaven—even wrongdoers seemed happy there at first, but it wasn't real.**

Moral: *Truth always reaches the highest, even when tested.*

- Even if it looks like you're suffering for being good, it's only a test.
- In the end, **truth wins**.
- **Real heaven** (peace, joy, inner happiness) belongs to those who stay loyal to truth, love, and dharma.
- Just like Yudhishthira, if you hold on to your values, you will reach the highest—no matter how hard the journey is.

Who is Krishna?

1. Krishna as Divine Energy (Shakti)
Krishna represents the active force behind all existence — the spark that powers creation and life.
Like electricity in a machine — invisible, yet essential.
Gita Echo: "I am the strength of the strong, free from desire and attachment." (7.11)

2. Krishna as the Soul (Atman)
He is the eternal presence within every being — the unchanging observer.
Like a steady flame inside a lamp, calm while the world flickers around it.
Gita Echo: "The Self is never born and never dies." (2.20)

3. Krishna as the Absolute (Brahman)
He is the limitless, formless reality behind all forms.
Like the deep ocean beneath its waves — steady, vast, and all-encompassing.
Gita Echo: "I am the foundation of the formless Brahman." (14.27)

4. Krishna as the Eternal (Sanatana)
Timeless and beyond the cycle of birth and death.
Like the sky, unchanged no matter what passes

through it.
Gita Echo: "I am unborn and imperishable." (4.6)

5. Krishna as Infinite (Ananta)
Boundless in all ways — in form, knowledge, and presence.
Like space — everything exists within it, yet it remains untouched.
Gita Echo: "My cosmic form has no beginning, middle, or end." (11.16)

6. Krishna as Divine Incarnation (Avatar)
He appears in form to restore balance when righteousness declines.
Like a healer who enters a sick body to cure it — purposeful and compassionate.
Gita Echo: "Whenever Dharma declines... I manifest." (4.7)

7. Krishna as God with Form (Saguna Brahman)
The divine made accessible — relatable and filled with qualities like love, wisdom, and strength.
Like white light splitting into a rainbow — one truth expressed in many ways.
Gita Echo: "The ignorant see Me as merely human, not knowing My true nature." (9.11)

8. Krishna as the Supreme Lord (Ishvara)
The master of the universe, guiding all from

within.
Like a conductor directing a symphony, unseen yet essential.
Gita Echo: "I dwell in the hearts of all beings." (10.20)

9. Krishna as the All-Attractive One (Bhagavan)
The complete expression of divinity — full of charm, wisdom, power, and love.
Like a magnet that draws hearts with divine love.
Gita Echo: "Out of compassion, I dispel darkness with the light of knowledge." (10.11)

10. Krishna as the Philosopher
The divine teacher of the Gita, merging paths of action, knowledge, love, and meditation.
Like a mirror revealing the true self; like a lamp lighting up confusion with clarity.

Key Messages:

- Life is a battlefield — face it with wisdom.
- Perform your duty without ego.
- The soul is eternal.
- True freedom comes through surrender, awareness, and devotion.

11. Krishna as the Charioteer
Though supreme, He chooses to serve — guiding Arjuna's chariot as a symbol of guiding

our lives.
The chariot = body, horses = senses, reins = mind, Arjuna = seeker, Krishna = inner wisdom.
Symbolic Lesson:

- God doesn't force, but waits for us to surrender the reins.
- Real guidance begins when we are willing to be led by higher wisdom.
- True leadership is service.

Krishna is **everything to every seeker** — the silent witness, the cosmic force, the beloved guide, and the infinite source. He is both beyond form and within reach, adapting Himself to the heart and understanding of the one who seeks Him.

Why some do not have faith in Krishna?

For Those Who Do Not Believe or Trust in Krishna

According to a spiritual guide, they do not see disbelief or a lack of trust in Krishna as something to be condemned. Rather, they see it as a phase in the soul's eternal journey. Every soul is on a unique path, and Krishna, in His infinite compassion, allows for all expressions of faith, doubt, seeking, and even denial.

Bhagavad Gita 4.11 beautifully says:

"Ye yathā māṁ prapadyante tāṁs tathaiva bhajāmy aham"
"As people approach Me, I reciprocate with them accordingly."

This verse teaches us that Krishna doesn't demand blind faith. He honors free will. He walks with the sincere seeker, whether they call Him Krishna, the Universe, Truth, or simply don't call Him at all.

What is their Faith, Then?

Even those who don't believe in Krishna **still believe in something**—whether it's science, self-effort, morality, human love, or logic. That **belief itself is a form of faith**. In the Gita (17.3), Krishna says:

"Shraddhā-mayo 'yaṁ puruṣo yo yacchraddhaḥ sa eva saḥ"
"A person is made of their faith. Whatever the nature of one's faith, that is what they become."

So even an atheist has **shraddha**—faith—in something. Their actions, values, and decisions are guided by that inner compass. The Gita recognizes this, dividing faith into **sattvic**, **rajasic**, and **tamasic** based on clarity, passion, or ignorance—not on which god is worshipped.

Why Do Some Not Believe in Krishna?

1. **Past experiences** – Pain, loss, or hypocrisy may have distanced them from devotion.
2. **Intellectual curiosity** – Some must question everything before accepting.
3. **Different karmic path** – Their soul may be destined to approach the truth in another way first.
4. **Aversion to form** – They may prefer the formless or universal aspect of divinity,

which is still Krishna in another expression.

Krishna accepts even these paths, as He says in **Gita 7.21**:

"Yo yo yām yām tanum bhaktaḥ śraddhayā arcitum icchati, tasya tasyācalāṁ śraddhāṁ tāṁ eva vidadhāmy aham" "Whichever form a devotee seeks to worship with faith, I make that faith steady."

Final Insight: Let the Flower Bloom in Its Time

According to a spiritual leader, we should not rush others to believe. Krishna is not insecure—He does not require forced devotion. He is patient, waiting silently in every heart, like the sun behind the clouds.

For some, the path to Krishna may be long. For others, He is recognized instantly. But no path is wasted. Every sincere step taken with awareness and love—be it through devotion, knowledge, karma, or questioning—leads eventually to the **same source**.

That's a truly important and delicate question, especially when approached from the standpoint of compassion and spiritual responsibility. As a spiritual guide, here's how I would lovingly and wisely address it:

Are Those Who Don't Believe in God on the Wrong Path?

Not necessarily. Everyone is on a **unique spiritual journey**. Just because someone does not believe in God **now** does not mean they are on the wrong path. It may be part of their **soul's growth**—a phase of learning through reason, experience, or even suffering. Krishna does not label people as "wrong" simply because they don't believe.

As **Bhagavad Gita 7.16** says, there are four kinds of people who turn to God—those in distress, those seeking knowledge, those desiring wealth, and those who are wise. But it never condemns those who haven't yet turned toward God. Instead, **it waits**—because the **Divine is always patient**.

Even doubt is sacred.

Doubt is the beginning of **real seeking**. A person who questions God sincerely is often closer to the truth than someone who worships without understanding.

How to Enlighten Them and Show the Right Path?

You do not need to argue or convince. The best way to help is to **live as an example**—through your peace, compassion, and clarity.

1. **Be a living inspiration.** When people see calmness, strength, and joy in you, they become curious. *"What gives her this peace?"* That curiosity is the beginning of faith.
2. **Speak the universal language.** Talk about love, truth, inner peace, and compassion—values that **even atheists believe in**. These are divine qualities.
3. **Introduce stories and metaphors.** Like the Bhagavad Gita does—use stories, symbols, and experiences to guide them inward. For example:

"A seed buried underground looks lost, but it's growing. So too, a soul in ignorance is silently evolving."

4. **Create safe spaces for dialogue.** Let them speak, doubt, question. The more

they open up, the more the inner self begins to awaken.

What Are the Consequences of Not Having Faith in God?

The consequences are not punishment—but **spiritual limitation** and inner suffering.

1. **Lack of inner anchoring:** Without faith in something higher, people may feel **lost, anxious, or purposeless**, especially during crises.
2. **Limited perspective:** They may rely only on their ego, logic, or material strength, which eventually fails. When faced with death, grief, or deep sorrow—they feel **isolated**.
3. **Karmic cycles:** Without surrender or spiritual awareness, they remain bound in the **cycle of karma**—chasing desires, suffering from disappointments, and missing the deeper purpose of life.
4. **Missed grace:** Faith invites **divine grace**, which helps us grow beyond our own limitations. Without it, life can feel like pushing a rock uphill alone.

Yet, even this suffering has a **divine purpose**—it eventually pushes the soul to ask, *"Is there* *something beyond all this?"* And that is when the real spiritual journey begins.

"You do not need to force people to believe in God. Instead, be the light that reminds them of the divine within themselves."

Every soul is like a lotus in the mud. Whether they believe or not, **they are still sacred**. Some bloom early, some late—but the sun (Divine) shines on all equally. Your role is to be the sunshine, the gentle rain, and the silent prayer.

How to Overcome Ego, Fear, Suffering, and Anger by Having Faith in Krishna

1. EGO (Ahamkara): Dissolved through Surrender

Ego says: *"I am the doer."*
Faith in Krishna says: *"I am an instrument."*

Bhagavad Gita 18.66:

"Sarva-dharmān parityajya māṁ ekaṁ śharaṇaṁ vraja"
"Abandon all duties and surrender unto Me alone."

When we truly **surrender**, ego begins to fade. Faith makes you realize that Krishna is the **doer**, the **knower**, and the **witness**. You're not here to control everything, but to align with **Dharma** and flow with His will.

Practice: Every day, say:

"Krishna, I am Yours. Use me for Your purpose. Not my will, but Thy will."

2. ANGER (Krodha): Healed through Devotion and Understanding

Gita 2.63 says:

"From anger comes delusion; from delusion, loss of memory; from loss of memory, the destruction of intelligence; and from the destruction of intelligence, one perishes."

When you trust Krishna, you understand that **everything happens for a reason**—according to karma and divine timing. You no longer take things personally. You don't react from ego, but respond from **compassion**.

Practice: When angry, chant:

"Om Shri Krishna Sharanam Mama"
Let your breath carry the anger away as you focus on His form.

3. FEAR (Bhaya): Melted through Trust in Krishna's Protection

Fear arises when we feel **alone and unprotected**. But Krishna says in **Gita 9.22**:

"To those who are constantly devoted and worship Me with love, I give the understanding by which they can come to Me. I protect what they have and carry what they lack."

Faith is the **armor** against fear. When you trust that Krishna is with you, even in darkness, fear vanishes like mist before the sun.

Practice: Repeat mentally:

"Krishna is with me, within me, around me. I fear nothing."

4. SUFFERING (Dukkha): Transformed through Bhakti and Wisdom

Suffering becomes unbearable when we think it is **meaningless**. But with Krishna, even pain becomes a **path to purification** and growth.

Gita 2.14:

"Matra-sparshas tu kaunteya shitoshna-sukha-duhkha-dah"

"O son of Kunti, the contact between the senses and the objects gives rise to cold and heat, pleasure and pain—they come and go. Endure them with patience."

Practice: In suffering, remember:

"Krishna, I accept this moment as Your will. Let it cleanse me. Guide me through it."

Let your pain become your prayer.

The essence: Bhakti Purifies All

When you offer your **mind, emotions, and actions to Krishna**, He purifies them all. Bhakti (devotion) is not weakness—it is the **highest strength**, because you allow divine love to wash away the lower nature.

Gita 12.13–14:

"He who is free from malice toward all beings, friendly and compassionate, free from possessiveness and ego, steady in pain and pleasure, forgiving, and ever content… such a devotee is dear to Me."

This is the **goal** and the **path**.

Final Message from a Spiritual Leader's Heart:

"Do not fight ego, fear, anger, or sorrow alone. Invite Krishna into your heart. Let His grace do the work. You don't need to become perfect to be close to Him—just be sincere. With faith, even your tears become offerings, your failures become fuel, and your life becomes divine."

Why does Krishna see all equally, even the thief?

Because Krishna sees the **soul**, not just the outer action.

- A **thief** may have done something wrong, but Krishna sees that the thief too is a **spark of the Divine**, just **confused**, lost in **maya (illusion)**.
- He sees the **potential** in every being to change, to rise, to become better.

It's like a teacher who **loves all students**, even the naughty ones — not because the wrong is right, but because **they too can learn and grow**.

Then, is the thief not punished?

He is — **through karma.**

- Krishna **doesn't interfere** with the **law of karma**.
- If a person steals, lies, or harms — **karma reacts** like a mirror.

- Krishna says, *"As you sow, so shall you reap."*
- So the **thief faces consequences**, not because Krishna punishes out of anger, but because **that's the law of the universe.**

Krishna's role is like the **sun** — it shines equally on all. Whether you use that sunlight to grow flowers or commit a crime, the **sun doesn't discriminate**, but **you'll face the result of your action**.

Analogy for kids (or anyone!):

Imagine a **school principal** who says,

"I love all students equally."
But when a child breaks the rule, they are sent to detention.
Still, the principal loves them and gives them **a chance to improve**.

That's Krishna — **just, fair, loving**, never hateful.

In the Gita, especially in Chapter 5 and Chapter 9, Krishna says:

"Samoham sarva-bhuteshu na me dveshyo 'sti na priyah."

(I am equal to all beings; I hate no one, nor am I partial to anyone.) – **Bhagavad Gita 9.29**

If no one catches the thief, how does he face consequences?

Because **karma is automatic** — like gravity.

Even if no one sees the act, **the universe has already recorded it**. Every thought, word, and deed creates a **vibration** and **imprint** in the soul.

3 Ways the Thief Faces Consequences Even Without Human Action:

1. Inner Guilt & Restlessness

Even if the world doesn't punish him, **his own conscience** does.

- He loses **peace of mind**.
- Sleeps with fear, suspicion, and anxiety.
- He starts becoming a slave to more lies, more hiding.

"The sinner punishes himself first — in his own heart."

2. Loss of Trust, Relationships, and Growth

- He may gain **temporary material benefit**, but loses **long-term respect**.
- People may sense something is off.
- Life creates **situations where his lies catch up**.

3. Karmic Reaction (Later Life / Next Life)

Karma works **beyond what we can see**.

- He may not be caught now, but later he may lose money mysteriously, face betrayal, illness, or even be **born in conditions where he suffers what he caused**.

Krishna says in Gita 4.17:
"Mysterious are the ways of karma."

Analogy: Planting a Poison Seed

If someone plants a **poisonous seed**, the result (the bitter fruit) **will come in time**, even if no one saw the seed being planted.

That's karma — **invisible at first, but certain**.

Krishna's Justice is Silent but Sure

He doesn't rush with punishment like a policeman. Instead, He allows each soul to:

- **learn through experience**
- **realize their own mistake**
- **grow from within**

Krishna sees the **divine light** in everyone, even the thief — and gives them **opportunities to rise**. But **karma ensures justice**.

How could Krishna have taught the Gita to the Sun god (Vivasvan) before being born as a human?

- Literal verse reference (Chapter 4, Verse 1):

"I taught this imperishable yoga to Vivasvan (the Sun God); Vivasvan taught it to Manu; Manu passed it on to Ikshvaku..."

- Spiritual Explanation:

Krishna is not just a human being in the Gita—he represents the **Supreme Consciousness** or **Eternal Divine**. From this perspective, Krishna is **not limited by birth and death**. His **true nature (Paramatma)** is beyond time. So, when he says he taught the Gita to the Sun god, it means the **eternal wisdom of dharma, karma,**

and self-realization has always existed and was passed on through divine forms before it was shared again in this human form.

- Modern Allegory for Kids

Imagine **Krishna as the "Internet of Wisdom"**—timeless, invisible, and always there. Sometimes, this wisdom connects to us through a phone (like a human body). Other times, it might connect through a computer (like the Sun god or a sage). Even if we only see the phone now, the internet existed before and can connect to anything at any time.

So, when Krishna says he taught the Gita to the Sun god, he means **this wisdom is ancient and universal**—it's just being "downloaded" again through him now.

- Moral for Students:

Wisdom is timeless. Even if it feels new to us, it has always existed in the universe, just waiting for the right moment and the right teacher to share it.

About The Author

Nagashwini N is a teacher, engineer, author, and entrepreneur, running Fancyritu Innovative Ideas and Hebbar Tuition and Training. With 9 years of software development experience, she writes and self-publishes books on Vedic philosophy, spirituality, education, career counseling, and creativity, selling them on online platforms. She also provides tuition for students from 4th to 10th grade. Skilled in web development, computer programming, and Vedic mathematics, she blends traditional wisdom with modern education. As an entrepreneur, she actively manages multiple home-based businesses while teaching students.

Her books serve as valuable resources for students, professionals, and spiritual seekers. They educate, inspire, entertain, and guide, making a significant impact on readers' lives. Whether someone is looking for academic support, career guidance, mental stimulation, or spiritual wisdom, her books provide the right knowledge and tools.

www.ingramcontent.com/pod-product-compliance
Ingram Content Group UK Ltd.
Pitfield, Milton Keynes, MK11 3LW, UK
UKHW021404190726
13845UKWH00028B/876

9 789334 278156